We Are Americans

VOICES OF THE IMMIGRANT EXPERIENCE

by Dorothy and Thomas Hoobler

SCHOLASTIC NONFICTION

⸙

To all those who helped make this book possible: our generous
friends in libraries, historical societies, and museums —
too many to list, but you know who you are! Many, many thanks.

⸙

For information regarding permission, write to Scholastic Inc.,
Attention: Permissions Department, 557 Broadway, New York, NY 10012.

Library of Congress Cataloging-in-Publication Data

Hoobler, Dorothy. ⸙ We are americans / by Dorothy and Thomas Hoobler. ⸙
p. cm. ⸙ Includes bibliographical references and index. ⸙ Summary: A history of
immigration to America, from speculation about the earliest immigrants to the
present day. ⸙ United States – Emigration and immigration – Juvenile literature.
[1. United States – Emigration and immigration.] I. Hoobler, Thomas. II. Scholastic
Nonfiction. III. Title. ⸙ JV 6450 .H66 2003 ⸙ 304.8'73 – dc21 ⸙ 2001049612

ISBN 0-439-16297-1

10 9 8 7 6 5 4 3 2   03 04 05 06 07

Printed in the U.S.A. 24

First printing, November 2003

Book design by Nancy Sabato ⸙ Composition by Kay Petronio and Nancy Sabato
Cover design by Kristen Ekeland

Title page photo credit: *Fourth of July Celebration in Centre Square* by John Lewis Krimmel
(The Historical Society of Pennsylvania). All other credits appear on pages 193-194.

CONTENTS

INTRODUCTION

A Japanese immigrant family poses for the camera around 1900 in Oregon.

An Italian immigrant girl sells newspapers on a New York City street.

"It was evening when our ship arrived in New York. . . . I spent the entire night on deck watching the thousands of lights of the city. I thought: This is the land I've traveled to. Here I'll find my father, my mother and my new sister. What will my young life change into in this new world? I sat and meditated the entire night long and didn't even try to go to bed."

These were the thoughts of Isaac Polvi, a young Finnish immigrant who came to the United States in the early 1900s. He wondered what his new life would be like. Other immigrants shared the feeling. It is part of the American experience.

All Americans are immigrants or descendants of immigrants. Our ancestors came here from all over the globe — on foot, by boat, train, bus, or airplane. Many new Americans are arriving today. The journey may be dangerous and difficult. But immigrants have always had a dream to guide them — the dream of America.

To those in the country they left behind, they were emigrants — people "going out." They had many reasons for leaving, reasons that historians call the push factor. Some were simply trying to escape poverty and lack of opportunity. Many were suffering persecution because of their religion or nationality or political beliefs. Many were literally fleeing for their lives, because invading armies or famine had overtaken their homelands. There were, and are today, some who sought adventure and a new life because they weren't satisfied with the one they had.

A Jewish immigrant girl waves the flag at a school assembly.

The attractions of the new country are called the pull factor. Those who came to the United States to settle, the immigrants, usually heard or read about America before they came. They might have received a letter from a friend or relative already there, or heard stories about the freedom and prosperity America offered.

To many, freedom was what the United States was all about. People could choose whatever work they had the talent to do, practice any religion, speak and write as they pleased. Opportunities were available. Immigrants had the same right to the riches of the country as the native-born.

The constant arrival of new people with courage, strength, and daring gave and still gives new energy to the country. Of course, conditions in the United States have sometimes been hard. Some newcomers have won great success, while others have experienced tragedy. But all immigrants brought to the new land their special skills and talents and ambition. As their lives were changed by crossing the border, so too would they change the country they came to call their own.

Families gather on the Fourth of July in a Mexican neighborhood of Chicago.

At a marriage of Slavic immigrants in Utah, the wedding party honors both their homeland and their new country.

CHAPTER ONE

THE FIRST IMMIGRANTS

"Ice had formed ahead of them, and it reached all the way to the sky. The people could not cross it. . . . A Raven flew up and struck the ice and cracked it. Coyote said, 'These small people can't get across the ice.' Another Raven flew up again and cracked the ice again. Coyote said, 'Try again, try again.' Raven flew up again and broke the ice. The people ran across."

This legend, told by the Paiute people of the Great Plains, describes a dangerous journey. In the story, Coyote, a source of wisdom in Paiute folklore, encourages people who are trying to cross an ice barrier. Many modern scholars believe that Native Americans came to America in just that way, long ago in prehistoric times. They were the first immigrants to America.

These immigrants went south toward a warmer climate and better hunting grounds. Conditions on their journey were terrible. The people traveled on foot because they had no transport animals. The cold and bitter winds whipping off the sides of huge glaciers stung their faces. Sometimes the sky was dark with volcanic ash. These travelers moved along valleys and narrow passes between mountainous glaciers. Their main route south is thought to have been along the eastern side of the Rocky Mountains and into the continental United States. From there, they spread east to the Atlantic Ocean and south to the tip of South America.

The first immigrants had no idea what lay ahead and probably had no particular destination in mind. They stopped when they found food and moved on when they needed more. And, of course, they came to an America where no other humans lived.

A priest of the Mandan people lifts a buffalo skull to the sky, asking for a successful hunt. Since ancient times, animals have played an important part in Native American culture.

Until very recently, most experts believed that the first Americans migrated from Asia. About 14,000 years ago, the world was in the midst of a cold period called the Last Ice Age. So much seawater became locked up in the glaciers that the sea level dropped more than 300 feet. The sea level was so low that Alaska and Siberia became connected. Scientists call this now-vanished land Beringia. Today Beringia is covered by a narrow strait of water that separates Alaska from Siberia, in Russia.

This Native American is demonstrating the use of an alt-alt. The alt-alt holds a spear and supplies added power and distance needed to bring down large game animals. Paleo-Indians used this device. This demonstration photograph was probably taken in the 1920s.

The people of Beringia hunted and fished, living in small bands. They made stone weapons to stab and cut their prey. Working together, groups of hunters went after big game, far larger than land animals of today. These hunters brought down the hairy mammoth, the giant mastodon with its gigantic tusks, and the fearsome saber-toothed tiger. The mammoths provided meat for food, their hides provided clothing, and their bones were used to build huts.

As the climate grew warmer, the sea level rose and started to flood Beringia. Eventually the tide broke through, forming the strait that separates Asia from America. Some people were stranded on the east side of the water, in America. Beringia disappeared 11,000 years ago. Over time, the people spread through North and South America.

NEW THEORIES

Today's scientists are challenging the old theory of a single migration across a land bridge from Siberia. New findings indicate that American immigrants arrived 20,000 years ago or even earlier.

Recent discoveries have also raised the possibility that there were several groups of early Americans — from different parts of the world. Perhaps America was a melting pot much earlier than anyone thought.

The oldest American skeleton yet discovered was found in Brazil. Given the nickname Luzia, it appears more Negroid (African) than Mongolian (Asian). In the United States, a mummified body found at Spirit Cave in Nevada resembles people from Southeast Asia and the Pacific Islands. In 1996 an ancient skull 9,500 years old was found in Kennewick, Washington; it resembles the skulls of Europeans more than Asians or Africans.

Some scientists now believe that many of the first Americans did not come on foot at all. They think these travelers migrated in animal-skin boats, hugging the shore along the Pacific coast from Asia to America. They may have established small communities along the coast. Through a leapfrogging process, using boats and walking, these early emigrants could have, over a long time, reached the tip of South America.

Some scholars think that hardy seafarers could have made it across the Atlantic Ocean from Europe to America long before Columbus. They also suggest that America's earliest inhabitants could have followed the ice surrounding Iceland and Greenland and then south to North America. Only new research and archeological finds will give us the answer to how the first humans came to America and who they were.

The Chinese "Discover" America

In A.D. 458, five Buddhist priests set sail from China. They traveled east past Japan and on across the Pacific. They sailed until they reached land in a northern kingdom that may have been Alaska. Their journey continued until they reached a lovely land with peaceful people. Some modern experts believe it was northern California. They spent more time in a kingdom farther south, which they called Fusang, believed to be in Mexico. The story of this marvelous journey comes from Hui-shen, a priest who wrote down the tale in A.D. 499. The account was preserved in the Chinese Imperial Archives.

More than 1,500 years later, another clue to an early Chinese voyage to America appeared. Monterey cypress trees grow along the coast of California; they are found nowhere else in North or South America. A naturalist took a branch of a Monterey cypress to the Panama-Pacific Exposition in San Francisco in 1915. There, a Chinese Buddhist identified the tree as the same as one that grows in China. Could the California tree have come from seeds the monks had brought from China? This would mean that the Chinese saw America very early indeed.

The hogan, or "home place," provided shelter for the Navajo people. Women did much of the work of putting the hogan together.

The Native Americans spread throughout the continental United States. They had to learn to live in deserts, mountains, plains, river valleys, and woodlands. As a result they developed many ways of life. But all these Native American societies shared a sense of harmony with nature. The people were conscious of how deeply linked humans were with other living creatures, and even with inanimate objects such as stones or water. "The landscape is our church," goes a Zuni saying. "It is like a sacred building to us."

Over time, the Native Americans in today's United States shifted from a hunting and gathering way of life to agriculture. Some learned to collect the seeds of wild plants to plant a crop the following year. Farther south in Mexico, people cultivated wild grasses into domestic corn. Corn could be made into bread, puddings, dumplings, and stews. Corn was so useful that many other people began to grow it. Tiny corncobs have been found in New Mexico that are at least 6,000 years old. By 200 B.C. corn was being grown as far north as Illinois.

THE DESERT CULTURE

Native Americans developed a very advanced desert agriculture in the Southwest. Around A.D. 300 the Hokoham people built a system of canals that stretched more than 500 miles throughout Arizona. About every three miles along the canals, they built villages encircled by walls. The Hokoham planted prickly cactus as hedges and a source of fruit. The water management achievements of the Hokoham would be copied centuries later by the city of Phoenix.

A neighboring desert people, the Anasazi, pioneered apartment living in the Americas. At Chaco Canyon in Arizona, they built houses that were a city block long. Some were five-story houses with more than one hundred rooms. The upper stories were reached with ladders, as there were no steps or hallways.

Another Anasazi center, at Mesa Verde in southwestern Colorado, sat on a 7,000-foot plateau with steep sides and had 600 cliff dwellings. The largest house was the Cliff Palace with 200 rooms. The people grew corn and beans on the mesa top. Shallow indentations in the rock enabled them to get a hold with their toes and fingers and climb up and down the vertical sides of the cliff.

THE MOUND BUILDERS

The mound-building culture is perhaps the most mysterious of the Native American civilizations. The mound builders lived along the Ohio and Mississippi rivers, in the middle of today's United States.

People used ladders to get inside these early "apartment houses" in Arizona.

Hiawatha and Deganiwidah

The fighting among the Iroquois threatened to get out of hand. A Huron named Deganiwidah canoed across Lake Ontario and preached a message of peace. When he landed on the southern shore, he was met by a Mohawk chief named Hiawatha. Hiawatha understood his message because he had lost all his daughters to tribal strife.

Deganiwidah spoke of using principles of justice and fairness to avoid bloodshed. The Peace Maker, as Deganiwidah was called, told Hiawatha of thirteen laws by which the people and tribes could live in peace. The laws contained ideas of democracy because they allowed participation of many in the decision-making of the tribe. One law was, look and listen for the welfare of the whole people and have always in view not only the present, but also the coming generations . . . the unborn of the future Nation.

Hiawatha became a supporter of the principles of Deganiwidah, and he spoke out powerfully to others. The two men traveled the Iroquois country forging alliances. They described the Tree of Peace, a white pine planted by Deganiwidah, under which members of each tribe would gather to discuss differences.

People carried thousands of baskets of earth to build mounds. The mounds were shaped in circles, squares, rectangles, or later, animal shapes. Burial chambers were often found in the heart of the mounds. The dead were surrounded by luxurious burial goods, such as carved tablets and decorative smoking pipes. In other places, pyramid buildings atop the mound became ceremonial and social centers for the living.

The "capital" of the mound-building culture was Cahokia, the first real city in the United States. Located near today's St. Louis, Cahokia had a population of more than 10,000 people. At the center of the city was an immense pyramid, today called Monk's Mount. It was the largest man-made prehistoric structure built anywhere — far larger than the Great Pyramid of Egypt. Its flattened top was the home of the ruler of the Cahokia empire, the Great Sun. The city's cedar posts were aligned to show the summer and winter solstices.

Cahokia was the center of a trade empire with a network of stations along the waterways that flowed through the center of today's United States. For some reason, Cahokia was abandoned around A.D. 1300. But mound building continued along some sites on the Mississippi until the arrival of the Europeans.

The Woodland Culture

Many different tribes lived in the Northeast. The woodlands contained wild fruit, nuts, and berries — cranberries, strawberries, raspberries, and grapes — as well as such edible plants as onions and fiddlehead ferns. In the spring, men tapped maple trees for their sap, which the women boiled down into a delicious syrup. Most of

The artifacts on this page were made by people of the mound-building culture.

The Native American Steam Bath

In 1655 Dutch settler David de Vries reported on the Native Americans living near New Amsterdam:

"When they wish to cleanse themselves of their foulness, they go in the autumn, when it begins to grow cold, and make, away off, near a running brook, a small oven, large enough for three or four men to lie in it. In making it they first take twigs of trees, and then cover them tight with clay, so that smoke cannot escape. This being done, they take a parcel of stones, which they heat in a fire, and then put in the oven, and when they think that it is sufficiently hot, they take the stones out again, and go and lie in it, men and women, boys and girls, and come out so perspiring, that every hair has a drop of sweat on it. In this state they plunge into the cold water, saying that it is healthy, . . . they then become entirely clean, and are more attractive than before."

the tribes grew corn as well. The streams were full of many varieties of fish, and shellfish was abundant in the ocean.

The most powerful of the woodland groups were the Iroquois tribes that lived in New York State. Called the Five Nations, they included the Seneca, Cayuga, Onondaga, Oneida, and Mohawk. Fighting was a way of life for the Iroquois. Wars broke out over hunting rights, over compensation for crimes, or just to take captives. The constant warfare threatened to weaken the Iroquois Nation. In the 1500s, just before the arrival of the Europeans, the Five Nations made an agreement to unite in a confederacy. Each nation retained full control over its own tribal affairs. But on issues that affected all the nations, they met and debated at the Grand Council. Each tribe had one vote and all agreements had to be unanimous, which meant that it sometimes took a long time to reach a consensus. But no one could be forced to go along with a decision. The colonial Americans from Europe were much impressed by this Iroquois custom. They used some of its features later for the government of the United States.

Canoes enabled Native Americans like this Chippewa family to navigate the river systems of North America. Boats like this were light enough to carry across land.

A Hairstyle with a Future

Many Europeans were impressed by the body painting and tattooing of the Native Americans. Both the French and the Dutch were startled by a Mohawk hairstyle where the head was shaved on both sides of the scalp and the hair across the top was made to stand up with the help of bear grease. This "Mohawk" would become a favorite of teenage boys hundreds of years later. Dominie Johannes Magalopensis, a minister of the Dutch Reformed Church at Albany, described it in 1642: "On the top of their heads they have a streak of hair from the forehead to the neck, about the breadth of three fingers, and this they shorten until it is about two or three fingers long, and it stands right on end like a cock's comb or hog's bristles; on both sides of this cock's comb they cut all the hair short, except the aforesaid locks, and they also leave on the bare places here and there small locks, such as are in sweeping-brushes, and then they are in fine array."

When Christopher Columbus set out on his first voyage in 1492, Europe had a strong society. Advances in science and military power gave Europeans a great advantage over the Native Americans. The Europeans arrived with guns, horses, and attack dogs — none of which the Native Americans had ever seen before.

The Native Americans had no defense against this terrifying force, which descended on them like a curse. One chief said, "Think, then, what must be the effect of the sight of you and your people, whom we have at no time seen, astride the fierce brutes, your horses, entering with such speed and fury into my country . . . things altogether new, as to strike awe and terror into our hearts."

Even more devastating for the Native Americans was their lack of immunity to European diseases. Illnesses such as smallpox and measles mowed people down by the tens of thousands. Malaria, typhus, cholera, and tuberculosis were silent killers that spread from tribe to tribe.

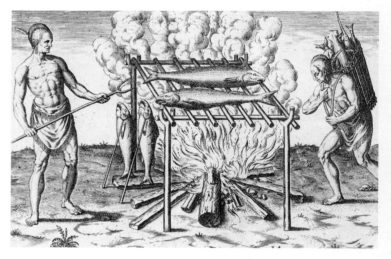

An early English visitor to what is now North Carolina drew this picture of the Native Americans' method of cooking fish.

The Delaware Indians described the strangeness of the Europeans in the tale of the arrival of Henry Hudson in 1609:

A great many years ago, when men with a white skin had never yet been seen in this land, some Indians who were out fishing, at a place where the sea widens, espied at a great distance something remarkably large floating on the water, and such as they had never seen before.

Some believed it to be an uncommonly large fish or animal, while others were of the opinion it must be a very big house floating on the sea. At length the spectators concluded that this wonderful object was moving towards the land, and that it must be an animal or something else that had life in it . . . runners soon after arriving declare that it is positively a house full of human beings, of quite a different color . . . that in particular one of them was dressed entirely in red, who must be the Mannitto himself.

In the centuries that followed, other tribes encountered European Americans. A young Navajo boy, Jaime, described his first sight of one: "I saw a man coming along with big white whiskers all over his face. The skin that showed was around his eyes, just a little bit. I had never seen a white man before. I ran away home and told the people I had seen something out there coming toward the sheep. It looked like a man, I said, but had wool all over its face. I thought the whiskers were wool, and I wasn't sure it was a man."

The arrival of the Europeans changed the Native Americans' way of life. The introduction of firearms made warfare between tribes far more deadly. Alcoholic drinks also caused disasters. The arrival of the horse, however, transformed the existence of many tribes for the better.

The greatest changes came to tribes on the Great Plains. The eastern Sioux, a canoeing people in 1760, adopted the horse as their means of transportation within thirty years. The mounted warrior of the Plains came to symbolize all Native Americans. A Cheyenne woman named Iron Teeth recalled: "My grandmother told me that when she was young . . . [t]he people themselves had to walk. In those times they did not travel far nor often. But when they got horses, they could move more easily from place to place. Then they could kill more of the buffalo and other animals, and so they got more meat for food and gathered more skins for lodges and clothing."

This mask of a bearded white man shows one early Native American view of a European.

"AMERICANIZING" THE FIRST AMERICANS

Over time, the growing numbers of European settlers, with their superior firepower, pushed the Native Americans into smaller and smaller areas. In the nineteenth century, tribes were placed on reservations, areas set aside for their use. These lands were poor in resources and isolated from the rest of the country. Agents appointed by the United States government had great power over the lives of Native Americans.

Many European Americans felt that it was necessary to "Americanize" these original Americans. They wanted to change their way of life by stamping out their values and customs, teaching them to adopt the ideals of their conquerors. Missionaries came to the reservations to make converts to Christianity. They condemned Native American religious practices, such as the ceremonies of the Sun Dance. Indian religious leaders were often expelled from the reservations and the telling of legends and myths was discouraged.

Young Native Americans were sent away to special boarding schools, such as the Carlisle Indian School in Pennsylvania. The school was founded by Captain Richard Pratt, who defined his goal for the young students as "Kill the Indian in him and save the man."

On entering such schools, the Native American children had their names taken away. Their hair was cut short and they were forced to discard their Indian clothing. Often, they were encouraged to make fun of their own culture. Martha Bercier, a Chippewa student, recalled the effect of one such school on her:

"Did I want to be an Indian? After looking at the pictures of the Indians on the warpath — fighting, scalping women and children, and Oh! such ugly faces. No! Indians are mean people — I'm glad I'm not an

These two pictures show the same person before and after he attended the Carlisle Indian School in the 1880s. He took the name Tom Torlino.

Learning How to Be White

The schools established by the United States government to teach Native Americans sought to "civilize" them by taking away their tradition and culture. Lone Wolf, a Blackfoot, described his school experience:

"School wasn't for me when I was a kid. I tried three of them and they were all bad. The first time was when I was about 8 years old. The soldiers came and rounded up as many of the Blackfeet children as they could. The government had decided we were to get White Man's education by force.

"It was very cold that day when we were loaded into the wagons. None of us wanted to go and our parents didn't want to let us go. Oh, we cried for this was the first time we were to be separated from our parents. . . . Nobody waved as the wagons, escorted by the soldiers, took us toward the school at Fort Shaw. Once there our belongings were taken from us, even the little medicine bags our mothers had given us to protect us from harm. Everything was placed in a heap and set afire.

"Next was the long hair, the pride of all the Indians. The boys, one by one, would break down and cry when they saw their braids thrown on the floor. All of the buckskin clothes had to go and we had to put on the clothes of the White Man.

"If we thought that the days were bad, the nights were much worse. This was the time when real loneliness set in, for it was then we knew that we were all alone. Many boys ran away from the school because the treatment was so bad but most of them were caught and brought back by the police. We were told never to talk Indian and if we were caught, we got a strapping with a leather belt."

Indian, I thought. Each day stretched into another endless day, each night for tears to fall. 'Tomorrow,' my sister said. Tomorrow never came. And so the days passed by, and the changes slowly came to settle within me. . . . Gone were the vivid pictures of my parents, sisters and brothers. Only a blurred vision of what used to be. Desperately I tried to cling to the faded past which was slowly being erased from my mind."

This training effectively cut these young people off from their communities and snuffed out their pride in their cultures. That pride was eloquently expressed by White Bear, a Kiowa chief: "I love the land and the buffalo, and will not part with it. . . . I want the children raised as I was. I don't want to settle. I love to roam over the prairies. There I feel free and happy. . . . This is our country. We have always lived in it."

CHAPTER TWO

COLONIAL IMMIGRATION

Richard Frethorne, who came to the Virginia colony
as a young man, wrote to his parents in England in 1623:

"Since I came out of the ship I never ate anything but peas, and loblollie [water gruel]. As for deer or venison I never saw any since I came into this land. There is indeed some fowl, but we are not allowed to go and get it, but must work hard both early and late for a mess of water gruel and a mouthful of bread and beef. . . . People cry out day and night — Oh! that they were in England . . ."

"And I have nothing to comfort me; there is nothing to be gotten here but sickness and death. . . . I have nothing at all — no, not a shirt to my back but two rags, nor no clothes but one poor suit. . . . My cloak is stolen by one of my own fellows, and to his dying hour [he] would not tell me what he did with it, but some of my fellows saw him have butter and beef out of a ship, which my cloak, I doubt [not] paid for. . . . I have eaten more in [one] day at home than I have allowed me here for a week. . . . For God's sake send beef and cheese and butter."

Obviously times were hard for Richard Frethorne — as they were for many of the nearly 1 million immigrants who came to the English colonies in America between 1607 and 1774. The climate of their new land was different from what they were used to. They had to build new homes and hunt or grow their own food. Like later immigrants, they felt uprooted. They might never again see their friends and family. Sea travel was difficult and dangerous in those days, and going to the colonies was seldom a round-trip journey.

The thirteen English colonies on the Atlantic Coast were not the only ones in today's United States. The Spanish had colonies along the Mississippi River and in today's Southeast and Southwest. French colonies ran from Canada through much of the midsection of North America. The English colonies, however, would set patterns that influenced the formation of the United States.

Arthur Szyk, a later Polish immigrant, painted this picture of the Poles who came to Jamestown in the very early years of the Virginia colony. They established the first factory for making glass.

21

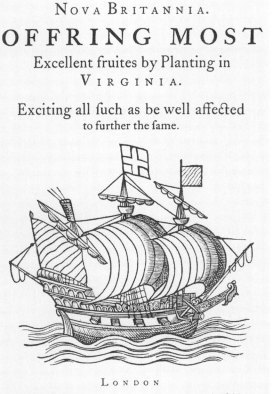

NOVA BRITANNIA.

OFFRING MOST

Excellent fruites by Planting in
VIRGINIA.

Exciting all such as be well affected
to further the same.

LONDON

Printed for SAMVEL MACHAM, and are to be sold at
his Shop in Pauls Church-yard , at the
Signe of the Bul-head.
1609.

The title page of an early English pamphlet encouraging people to go to the English colony in Virginia.

Virginia was the first permanent English colony. In 1607, 105 settlers, all male, came to a place they called Jamestown, near the Chesapeake Bay. Like many immigrants who followed, they were looking for riches and adventure. Few of them thought of settling there permanently. They were so unprepared for the hard life that many died in the early years, and several times the colony was on the brink of breaking up. The colony survived its first year only because Captain John Smith, a farmer's son, took control. Smith's first rule: "He who does not work does not eat."

To persuade settlers to leave home, the London Company offered three acres of Virginia land and ship's passage to anyone willing to work for four to seven years. These settlers were called *indentured servants,* because the agreement that bound them to work was an indenture.

The American tradition of representative government started in Virginia. In 1619 the colony established the House of Burgesses, the first legislative assembly in North America. Among the laws it passed was one that gave Polish-born colonists the same legal rights as any other resident. That opened the door for people of many nations to come to America and obtain citizenship.

The year 1619 was significant for another reason: The first Africans arrived in Virginia. At the beginning they were treated like indentured servants. Over time, they would become a slave labor force and be the only immigrants to be brought against their will.

MASSACHUSETTS

Far to the north, another permanent colony began in Massachusetts in 1620. Its founders, called Pilgrims, came as families, and they intended to settle there for good. They believed they were on a spiritual

The Pilgrims' First Winter

William Bradford described the Pilgrims' terrible first winter in 1620–1621.

"In two or three months time, half of their company died, especially in January and February, being the depth of winter, and wanting houses and other comforts, [and] being infected with the scurvy and other diseases which this long voyage . . . had brought upon them. So as there died some times two or three a day in [this] time, of one hundred and odd persons, scarce fifty remained. And of these, in the time of most distress, there were but six or seven sound persons, who, to their great commendation . . . spared no pains, night or day, but with abundance of toil and hazard of their own health, fetched wood [for those who were ill], made them fires, [prepared] them meat, made their beds, washed their loathsome clothes, clothed and unclothed them."

mission. The Pilgrims were English Protestants who did not accept the official Church of England. They were the first to come to the colonies to seek religious freedom.

A total of 102 passengers crossed the Atlantic on the ship *Mayflower*, landing at Plymouth in 1620. Before the Pilgrims came ashore they agreed to live according to a set of rules; the agreement became known as the Mayflower Compact. It became a model for the governments of other New England towns.

After 1628 another group of English settlers came to Massachusetts — the Puritans. They founded the Massachusetts Bay Colony farther north of Plymouth. Like the Pilgrims, the Puritans opposed the Church of England. But they wanted to reform, or purify, the church from within — thus their name.

The Pilgrims gave thanks for their safe arrival when they landed at Plymouth in 1620.

Sweden's Colony in the New World

In 1655 the Dutch from New Amsterdam took over the Swedish colony that lay south at the site of today's Wilmington, Delaware. The first settlers had come in 1638 and built Fort Christina, naming it after the Swedish queen. Many of the settlers were actually Finns. Finland was then under Swedish rule. Some of them were prisoners who had been found guilty of chopping trees in the royal orchards. They were given the choice of emigrating or hanging.

The third Swedish governor was Johan Printz, who weighed almost 400 pounds. (The Native Americans called him "Big Belly.") During his rule, the number of residents increased with the arrival of bonded servants. The Finns and Swedes introduced the classic log cabin and the sauna to the American colonies.

Like the Pilgrims, the Puritans looked to the New World as a place of rebirth. As John Winthrop, a Puritan leader, gazed upon the New World from his ship, he wrote words of advice: "For we must consider that we shall be as a City upon a Hill, the eyes of all people are upon us." In other words, the Puritans must become an example for all people. This was their "errand into the wilderness": to found a better and "new" England. In the centuries that followed, other Americans would come to see their nation as that shining example for the rest of the world.

These first two colonies set certain patterns for the English language, the right to representative government, and the importance of community. Later immigrants would adopt these patterns as part of becoming American.

NEW YORK

The third model colony was originally not English at all. In 1624 thirty families sent by the Dutch West India Company landed on Manhattan Island. Peter Minuit, a German acting for the company,

The first Africans in the English colonies arrived in Jamestown in 1619.

bought the island from some Native Americans for twenty-four dollars' worth of goods. It was dubbed New Amsterdam, after the capital of the Dutch Republic.

From the beginning, New Amsterdam was a colony of many nationalities. Many of the first thirty colonial families in New Amsterdam were Protestant Belgians. The colony also attracted settlers from Norway, Denmark, and Sweden, who often came as sailors. One of the Danes was Jonas Bronck, who bought farmland north of Manhattan and gave his name to today's New York City borough of the Bronx. In 1643 Isaac Jogues, a French Jesuit missionary, visited the city. He was amazed by the range of people he saw. He counted eighteen languages being used in the city, including Polish, Czech, Italian, German, English, and French.

In 1654, twenty-three Sephardic Jews arrived in New Amsterdam. Peter Stuyvesant, the governor of New Amsterdam, was at first unwilling to let the refugees stay in his colony. However, the directors of the Dutch West India Company ordered Stuyvesant to allow the refugees to stay and practice their religion. They formed the first Jewish community in what is now the United States.

The ship *Sainte Catherine* brought the first Jewish community to New Amsterdam, today's New York City. The passengers came from Brazil in 1654, fleeing persecution.

This indenture was for Isaac Hutton, age twelve. He became an apprentice who would learn the trades of goldsmith, silversmith, and jeweler.

The rulers of the English colonies continually sought more people to do the work the colonies needed to grow. Europe's frequent wars caused misery and gave a strong push to anyone inclined to go to America. Opportunities for land and work, as well as the chance to start a new life, would provide the pull factor to the colonies.

Shipowners and colonial governments sent agents called *newlanders* around Europe to talk up the New World. Usually well-dressed, they told stories of servant maids becoming ladies and men acquiring land and becoming rich.

But the best ads for the colonies were letters from settlers. "It is as good a country as any man needs to dwell in, and it is much better than I expected it to be in every way," an Irish immigrant from Belfast wrote home. Gabriel Thomas, a Welsh immigrant, even claimed that babies born in the colonies were without "blemishes" and that they were "more tender in heart" than other babies.

THE TRIP

Sailing to America was dangerous, expensive, and uncomfortable. The journey could take six weeks to six months, though three months was the average. Shipowners packed men, women, and children like sardines in the small spaces between the decks, which were rarely more than five feet high. The food was terrible and often insufficient for the long trip. Biscuits frequently had spiders and red worms in them. The living quarters stank from vomit, sweat, and human waste.

For the privilege of enduring these hideous conditions, passengers had to pay high ticket prices. They often paid for their passage through varieties of the indenture system. A person signed a contract before leaving Europe, pledging to work from four to seven years. Children usually had to serve until they were twenty-one. At the end

A German Redemptioner
Arrives in America

Johann Carl Buettner was born in the village of Lauta in southern Germany. He came to Philadelphia as a redemptioner (similar to an indentured servant) in the 1770s. He wrote of his arrival:

"We anchored amid stream in the river and took delight in gazing at the beautiful city of Philadelphia. On the following day, we were led to a building in the city where we took the oath of allegiance to King George II of England, under whose control at the time the North American territory was. As we put our feet on land, on coming from the ship, the earth seemed to sway beneath us and we staggered like drunken men. . . .

"After we had taken the oath of allegiance to the king of England, we were obliged to return to the boat. Shortly after, an announcement [was made] in the American newspapers: 'That a boat at present lying in the harbor of Philadelphia had arrived from Europe carrying a load of male and female persons, and that whoever might wish to purchase some of them, was invited to visit the boat.' Shortly afterwards, professional men arrived from the cities and owners of plantations from the country, who bargained with the ship's captain for our persons. We had to strip naked, so that the prospective purchasers could see that we had perfectly developed and healthy bodies. After the purchaser had made a selection, he asked: 'How much is this boy or this girl?' Many strong and healthy young men, and especially the pregnant women brought as much as sixty pounds sterling [three hundred dollars]. The captain asked for me thirty pounds sterling and I had to bind myself for the term of six years. . . . The master who paid this money for me . . . was the owner of a plantation in the province of New Jersey, and a member of the religious sect of Quakers."

of their indenture term, they usually got "freedom dues." These might include clothing, a year's supply of food, an ax or hoe, and often some land. At least half of the white immigrants during colonial times came as indentured servants.

On arrival, the indentured servants couldn't leave the ship until their fare was paid. Merchants and others looking for workers boarded the vessel at the dock, examining the human cargo. They felt young men's muscles, looked at people's teeth, and otherwise judged whether they could withstand the rigors of hard work and long hours. It was like a cattle sale.

Ship captains advertised the availability of their passengers who needed to become indentured servants in order to pay for their tickets.

Irish Servants.

JUST ARRIVED, *in the* Ship JOHN, *Capt.* ROACH, *from* DUBLIN,
A NUMBER of HEALTHY, INDENTED
MEN and WOMEN SERVANTS:
AMONG THE FORMER ARE,
A Variety of TRADESMEN, with some good FAR-
MERS, and stout LABOURERS: Their Indentures will be disposed
of, on reasonable Terms, for CASH, by
GEORGE SALMON.
Baltimore, May 24, 1792.

Germans came from all over Europe. These emigrants were leaving Salzburg in today's Austria for Georgia.

WHERE THEY CAME FROM

In the 1600s the largest number of colonists came from England. By the turn of the next century, however, most newcomers to America were Protestants from northern Ireland. They were actually Scots-Irish — people of Scottish descent who had settled in Ireland. Scots came from Scotland as well. In colonial times, Catholic Irish came to America in lesser numbers. Many went to Maryland, a colony that was founded as a refuge for Catholics.

Even before the American Revolution, immigrants arrived from all over the European continent. French Huguenots — who were Protestant — came fleeing religious persecution by the French monarchy. The Huguenots tended to be highly skilled workers, and the English colonies were glad to get them.

Germans formed the largest European immigrant group from outside the British Isles. At the time, there was not one country of Germany. Instead there were more than 300 German-speaking states and independent cities, most of them quite small. The German people suffered from continual warfare, religious oppression, and poverty. They looked to America for a more peaceful existence.

AFRICANS IN COLONIAL TIMES

Enslaved Africans were the unwilling immigrants of colonial times. They formed the largest population group in the colonies except for the British. Most enslaved Africans came from the west coast of Africa. They had been kidnapped from

Africans were shackled before being loaded on ships for the colonies. They sailed in terror to an unknown future.

A Slave Bears Witness

Olaudah Equiano was enslaved in Africa and shipped across the Atlantic as a boy of ten in 1765. He described the horrors of the crossing in his autobiography:

"The first object which saluted my eyes when I arrived on the coast was the sea, and a slave ship which was then riding at anchor and waiting for its cargo. These filled me with astonishment, which was soon converted into terror when I was carried on board. I was immediately handled and tossed up to see if I were sound by some of the crew, and I was now persuaded that I had gotten into a world of bad spirits and that they were going to kill me.

"I was soon put down under the decks, and there received such a salutation in my nostrils as I had never experienced in my life: so that with the loathsomeness of the stench and crying together, I became so sick and low that I was not able to eat. . . . I now wished for the last friend, death, to relieve me; but soon, to my grief, two of the white men offered me eatables, and on my refusing to eat, one of them held me fast by the hands . . . and tied my feet while the other flogged me severely. I had never experienced anything of this kind before, and although, not being used to the water, I naturally feared that element the first time I saw it, yet nevertheless could I have got over the nettings I would have jumped over the side."

their homes or were captives in intertribal fighting. African kings sold them for rum, guns, cloth, and other trade articles. The captives were usually roped together and marched to the coast, where they were sold to slave traders. Most of them had never seen the ocean before. When they saw the ships, many desperately tried to claw their way back to the beach to avoid the trip. Their captors often beat them with whips and clubs to get them aboard.

The trip on a slave ship was a voyage from hell. The men were chained in pairs and packed tightly between decks. Women often went unchained but they, too, were packed in as tightly as possible. On days with good weather, the slaves were brought on deck so that they could get air. Some captains did not permit this, for too many slaves tried to throw themselves overboard, preferring drowning to being sent back below deck. It was not uncommon for one fourth of the slaves to die during the voyage. Sharks followed the slave ships, waiting for the next body to be thrown overboard.

The Founding of Philadelphia

No one was a greater booster of America than the English Quaker William Penn. In 1681 King Charles II granted a tract of land in America to Penn, who wanted to create a haven for Quakers. Penn wrote pamphlets showing Pennsylvania with smiling Indians and crops that never failed. Among his selling points for the colony were religious freedom, the right of all (male) colonists to vote, and the lack of any compulsory military service. This last was important, for it was a time of frequent warfare in Europe, and young men were often dragged from their homes and families to serve in the armies.

In 1682 Penn came to America and laid out the city of Philadelphia. The colony grew quickly, partly because of its freedoms. In 1683 alone, more than thirty ships brought several thousand settlers. Throughout the colonial period, Philadelphia would take in more immigrants than any other American city.

By 1750 the English colonies were very much a multicultural community, though the English influence remained important. British-born or people of British descent made up two thirds of the white population. The language, legal system, and form of government were based on British models.

But colonial America was not a replica of England. Its non-English citizens put their own imprint on the country, just as later ones would do. Germans brought foods like mashed potatoes and apple pie and such customs as the Christmas tree. (The English Puritans banned Christmas celebrations and made it a point to work on that day.) The French Huguenots influenced others with their style and elegance. French dancing masters were much in demand by wealthy families. The Dutch contributed words to the American language like *cookie, boss, sleigh, coleslaw,* and *snoop.* The Boston minister Cotton Mather learned from his African slave the West African trick of inoculating people with smallpox to prevent them from catching the disease. Mather was ridiculed when he tried it, but its effectiveness soon won acceptance of the practice. Africans also taught their masters in South Carolina the secrets of growing rice.

The Dutch settlers in New York dressed up and greeted friends on New Year's Day.

In the English colonies, people of many religions practiced their faiths openly. This was unusual in Europe, and indeed in most of the rest of the world. Dr. Alexander Hamilton, a Scottish physician, wrote in the middle of the eighteenth century that he had dined at a tavern in Philadelphia "with a very mixed company of different nations and religions. There were Scots, English, Dutch, Germans, and Irish; there were Roman Catholics, [Anglican] Church men, Presbyterians, Quakers, Newlightmen, Methodists, Seventh Day men, Moravians, Anabaptists, and one Jew." He was surprised that such a diverse company could sit down together without quarreling.

Even so, there was some religious discrimination in the colonies. The most disliked religion was Roman Catholicism. Catholics made up only 1 percent of the population. In some colonies they were not allowed to hold office. Even in Maryland, which had been established as a haven for Catholics, they were soon discriminated against. People in Massachusetts celebrated Guy Fawkes Day (the anniversary of the

Jumping over a broomstick was part of the African-American wedding ritual. The musician is playing a banjo, an African instrument.

discovery of a Catholic plot to blow up the king and parliament) by burning effigies of the pope.

Many colonists preserved the customs and traditions they had brought with them. Among these was language. The Germans were the largest group of non-English speakers, and some Germans never bothered to learn English at all. In heavily populated Pennsylvania, Germans set up their own schools where children were taught in their native language. Christopher Dock, a teacher in one such school, used a blackboard, chalk, and erasers as teaching tools, starting a practice that continues today. Germans also had their own native-language newspapers, just as many immigrant groups still do. Immigrants

Scots from Scotland and Ireland were usually Presbyterians. These eighteenth-century worshippers are celebrating services outdoors.

Prejudice in Colonial America

Though America was a diverse society, prejudice against groups perceived as "different" was common. National stereotypes could be vicious. Benjamin Franklin disliked the Irish, whom he called "a low and squalid class of people." Dr. Andrew Hamilton, himself an immigrant from Scotland, found the Dutch in Albany "both old and young . . . remarkably ugly . . . in their persons slovenly and dirty." Charles Woodmason called the Scots-Irish "very Poor owning to their indolence. . . . They delight in their present low, lazy, sluttish, heathenish, hellish life. . . . Both Men and Women will do anything to come at Liquor, Cloaths, Furniture, &tc, &tc, rather than work for it."

The French faced prejudice during the wars between England and France. Even though the French in the English colonies were Protestant, they were suspected of double loyalty. In 1692 during King William's War (a conflict between the English and French colonies in America), a mob attacked and destroyed the Huguenot settlement of Frenchtown, Rhode Island. Many Huguenots were arrested even in tolerant Pennsylvania. South Carolina threatened Huguenots with loss of their estates upon their deaths, on the grounds that they were foreigners.

In Pennsylvania, where Germans made up one third of the population, many people resented their success. The way Germans clung to their native language seemed particularly irritating to English speakers. Benjamin Franklin complained, "Few of their children . . . know English. They import many books from Germany. . . . They will soon so outnumber us, that all the advantages we have, will . . . be not able to preserve our language, and even our government will become precarious."

also formed organizations based on their national group — another practice that still continues.

After 1725 the majority of the population was American-born for the first time. This American majority would set standards they expected new immigrants to adhere to. Of course, some immigrants chose to blend in with the majority because they were proud of becoming citizens, glad to have greater rights than they did in their home countries, or for social and business reasons.

In 1740 the British parliament granted citizenship to anyone who had lived in the colonies for five years. So from the beginning American citizenship did not depend on nationality. Anyone could become an American. Such a liberal citizenship policy encouraged more immigration, and it would have far-reaching effects on the nation after independence.

The French explorer René-Robert Cavelier, Sieur de LaSalle landed a small band of colonists at Matagordo Bay in today's Texas. The colony failed.

The first French settlement in America was established in 1604, three years before Jamestown. It was a fishing community near the border of today's Maine and Canada. In 1608 Samuel de Champlain built a fort at Quebec overlooking the Saint Lawrence River, the gateway to the interior of the continent. From there, future explorers and missionaries made their way to the Great Lakes and down the Mississippi River and its tributaries to the Gulf of Mexico. They called this territory Louisiana, after the King of France.

From Detroit in the north to New Orleans in the south, the French established a chain of settlements where they exchanged goods for furs with the Native Americans. The fur trade became New France's main economic activity.

FINDING SETTLERS

New France would occupy a much larger area than the English colonies, which clustered close to the Atlantic coast. However, France never managed to densely populate its North American territory, even though France itself had the largest population of the colonial powers of Europe.

One reason was religious intolerance. King Louis XIV of France, a staunch Catholic, banned Protestants called Huguenots from going to the French colonies in America. As a result, France lost these talented people to the English colonies.

Few ordinary French people or families were interested in emigrating to America. Merchants and government agents called *intendants* rounded up a small number of them — usually poor and landless laborers. Military recruits and prisoners paroled from jails made up a large number of the settlers. The intendants took their recruits before a magistrate, and had them sign a paper like an indenture. The emigrant, or *engagé,* thus was bound to a specific person for whom he or she had to work for a specified number of years. After fulfilling their contracts, the *engagés* became traders or farmers, called *habitants.*

The largest settlement in Louisiana was founded as New Orleans in 1718. This city became the center where sugar and cotton planters shipped their goods. Much of the labor was done by slaves, and Africans made up more than 10 percent of the city's population.

New Orleans grew rapidly. Within ten years of its founding, Capuchin friars opened parish schools for boys, and Ursuline nuns opened an academy for girls. In 1728 so-called casket girls started to arrive from France. They were orphans or daughters of French peasants. The Ursuline nuns cared for them until they were married.

The First Asian-American Community

The first Asian community in the United States was populated by Filipinos who settled on the outskirts of New Orleans in 1763. The founders were Filipino sailors called "Manilla Men," who sailed on Spanish galleons making the regular run between the Philippines and Mexico. A small number jumped ship at Acapulco and fled northward to escape Spanish rule. They settled in the swampy Louisiana bayous, where they felt safe from discovery and capture. Since they were all men, they intermarried with the Cajuns already living there. Later they intermarried with Indians, Irish, and Spanish. Their homes, on stilts in the swamps, could only be reached by canoes. Over time, their largest village, Saint Malo, became a thriving fishing community. These Filipino settlers introduced the Philippine tradition of drying shrimp on platforms, which preserved them in a day when there was no refrigeration.

An Illinois chief called explorer Enrico Tonti "Iron Hand" because he had a steel claw in place of a hand as a result of a war injury.

SPANISH COLONIES

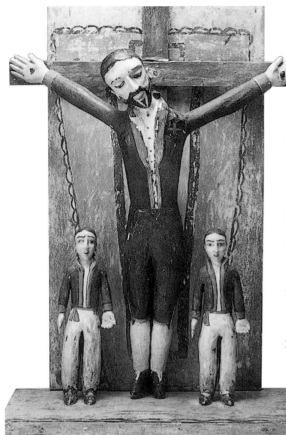

People in the Southwest created religious folk art called santos. People prayed to them for help and protection.

The Spaniards established the first permanent settlement in today's United States at Saint Augustine, Florida, in 1565. Spain's control spread over the Southeast from Florida to Georgia and Alabama. Its first settlement west of the Mississippi River was Santa Fe, founded in 1610. The Spanish colonial approach was different from the English one. The colonies were run from Spain, with little self-government by the colonists. Decisions of the most minute type were made in Madrid, the capital of Spain. Also, no religious views other than Roman Catholicism were tolerated either at home or in the colonies.

Having no dissenting religious group cut down the number of Spanish immigrants who wished to go to the New World. But Spain did have many ambitious men who wanted to make their fortunes in America and priests who wanted to save souls by converting Native Americans. Spain sent soldiers and priests to the New World rather than families. Since the number of Spanish settlers were few, as well as mostly male, they intermarried with the Indians; their children formed a *mestizo* population.

Throughout the Southeast and Southwest, the mission system was the main Spanish method of colonization. The center of the settlement was the church and the *presidio,* or fort. Priests converted the Indians and soldiers protected them.

Santa Fe's first governor complained that "no one comes to America to plant and sow, but only to eat and loaf." Native American labor built the churches and houses for the new settlement. The natives also became the bell ringers, organists, cooks, and gardeners in the missions. They learned Spanish methods of carpentry, blacksmithing, and masonry. The missions had farms and schools as well as churches. Spanish monks were among the founders of today's San Antonio,

El Paso, Santa Fe, Tucson, San Diego, Los Angeles, Monterey, and San Francisco. The Spanish brought peach trees and watermelons to Georgia; domestic animals such as horses, cattle, sheep, goats, and chickens to the Southeast and Southwest; and introduced the use of tools such as cart wheels, saws, nails, and chisels.

The most familiar legacy of the Spanish colonists was the work of the *vaquero,* the men who tended the cattle. From high-heeled boots to wide-brimmed hats, the vaqueros' outfits were adopted by cowboys throughout the American West. Their vocabulary became part of the language of the United States. *La riata,* or rope, became a lariat. An untamed horse was a *mustañero* in Spanish, a mustang in English. The vaqueros invented the rodeo, or summer roundup of cattle to be divided among their owners. At these events, the Spanish cowhands displayed their skills, competing to see who was best.

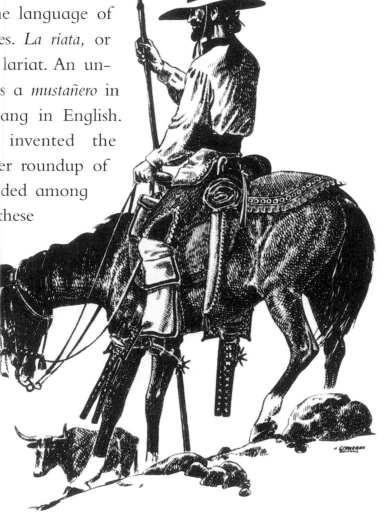

The vaqueros tended cattle in the Spanish colonies. Much of their equipment and techniques were later copied by American cowboys.

Father Junípero Serra

The man who built the first permanent settlement in California was born Miguel José Serra in 1713 on the island of Mallorca, which was part of Spain. At sixteen he entered the Franciscan order and took the name Junípero.

When Serra was thirty-seven, he volunteered to go to the New World to serve in the missions the Franciscans were founding. Father Serra worked in north-central Mexico until 1769 when he went north with the explorer Gaspar de Portola and began to build missions in present-day California. His first was named San Diego de Alcala, the foundation of today's city of San Diego.

Father Serra founded nine missions in all. The northernmost was San Francisco de Asís, where the city of San Francisco now stands. His idea was to have each mission be about a day's walk from the next one. Father Serra made his headquarters at San Juan de Capistrano; the chapel where he said Mass is today the oldest building in California.

Working tirelessly to convert Native Americans to Christianity, Father Serra also introduced methods of agriculture and irrigation.

CHAPTER THREE

WHAT IS AN AMERICAN?

"What then is the American, this new man? He is either a European or the descendant of a European; hence that strange mixture of blood which you will find in no other country. I could point out to you a family whose grandfather was an Englishman, whose wife was Dutch, whose son married a French woman, and whose present four sons have . . . four wives of different nations. He is an American who, leaving behind him all his ancient prejudices and manners, receives new ones from the new mode of life he has embraced, the new government he obeys, and the new rank he holds. . . . Here individuals of all nations are melted into a new race of men whose labors and posterity will one day cause great changes in the world."

The famous question "What is an American?" was asked — and answered — by the French-born Michel-Guillaume-Jean de Crèvecoeur. After coming to the colonies in 1759, he eventually became a naturalized citizen. Ten years later he bought a farm in New York State. While living there, he wrote *Letters from an American Farmer,* which was published in 1782. Crèvecoeur defined Americans as a people created from many European nations. His writings were the first expression of the "melting pot" ideal of American identity. This metaphor compared America to a pot in which many different elements are mixed and blended together into something new.

The idea that an American was a new type of person reflected the hopes and dreams of the new nation that the American Revolution created. In the years that followed, the new United States would offer opportunity for immigrants. Immigrants, in return, would help the nation expand both in territory and wealth. Between 1790 and 1815 about a quarter million European immigrants came to the United States. Many would leave a permanent mark on their adopted country.

Immigrant John Lewis Krimmel painted this picture of a Fourth of July celebration in Philadelphia. It shows the diversity of people who took pride in being Americans. (detail)

From War, a New Nation

Philip Mazzei was a neighbor of Thomas Jefferson. His ideas and writings affected the Declaration of Independence.

By 1775 the colonies had a population of about 2.5 million. The colonists were in a heated dispute with Britain about taxes. The colonials argued that since they had no representation in the British Parliament, they should not have to pay taxes that Parliament levied on them.

Some colonials felt it was time that the colonies gained independence. Thomas Paine, a corset maker and recent immigrant, produced the strongest arguments for separation from Britain. In his pamphlet *Common Sense,* published in early 1776, he pointed out that the colonies got no benefits from being part of the British imperial system. Paine asserted that loyalty to Britain was misplaced, because "Europe and not England is the parent country of America."

On July 4, 1776, the delegates to the Continental Congress in Philadelphia voted for independence. The rousing words of liberty in the Declaration of Independence attracted attention throughout the world and thrilled people seeking liberty: "We hold these truths to be self-evident, that all men are created equal . . ." The ideals of freedom were never stated better, and they would draw people to fight for the cause of independence.

The French noble Marquis de Lafayette, a young man of twenty, contributed his personal fortune as well as his military skills to the struggle. From Germany came Baron Wilhelm von Steuben, who helped to turn the American troops into an orderly, efficient fighting force. Then fifty years old, he suffered through the hard winter of 1777–1778 with Washington's troops at Valley Forge.

Two Polish volunteers came to assist the cause. Tadeusz Kosciuszko arrived in 1777 and helped to defeat the British at the crucial battle of Saratoga the next year. Kazimier Pulaski announced on his arrival, "I came to hazard all for the freedom of America." He did indeed give his life for the cause at the Battle of Savannah in 1779.

IMMIGRANT CONTRIBUTIONS

More than one third of General Washington's army were immigrants. Most of the immigrant soldiers were Irish-born. Indentured servants were drawn to the Continental Army by a promise of freedom and thirteen acres of land after the war. On the night before Saint Patrick's Day in 1776, American soldiers moved quickly and quietly toward Boston. By morning Boston was surrounded, and the British abandoned it. That night's password — chosen by George Washington himself — was "Saint Patrick."

Germans were also important to the American side, both as soldiers and gunsmiths. The long rifle developed among the Pennsylvania Germans was the finest and most accurate weapon of its time.

Wars cannot be fought without money. Haym Solomon, a Polish Jew, helped to

Baron von Steuben, the "drill-master" for General Washington, took over the training of soldiers at Valley Forge.

When Congress ended the slave trade in 1807, it was cause for celebration for African Americans.

Grand Celebration!
THE ABOLITION OF THE SLAVE TRADE
GENERAL ORDER.

raise more than six hundred and fifty thousand dollars to equip the American troops and keep the government afloat. That was a fortune at the time, worth many millions of dollars today. Solomon was never repaid the money.

The American victory created a new independent nation, now made up of thirteen states instead of colonies. During the struggle, the participants, both immigrant and native-born, forged a sense of common destiny. No longer were they just transplanted English or Europeans, but a new kind of people — Americans. All Europeans who had fought for the side of independence were granted citizenship, no matter when they had come.

THE NEW GOVERNMENT

When delegates from the states met in Philadelphia in

1787 to write a constitution, they dealt with only one form of immigration — the slave trade. The delegates agreed that Congress could end the slave trade after twenty years. Congress did so in 1807. From that time, only a small number of Africans were forcibly brought into the country, and they were the first illegal entrants.

The founders thought deeply about what it was to be an American, a citizen of the United States. What would be the *rights* of the immigrants? Should they be the same as the native-born? Alexander Hamilton, born on the Caribbean island of Nevis, argued in favor of encouraging immigration and giving immigrants the same level of citizenship as the native-born. Another immigrant delegate, James Wilson of Scotland, noted that if immigrants could help frame the Constitution itself, they should be able to serve in any political office.

The framers of the Constitition decided that any immigrant who became a citizen and met a residency requirement would be eligible for all the nation's political offices *except* the presidency. The president had to be a native-born citizen of the United States. An immigrant could serve in the House of Representatives, but only after he had been a citizen for seven years. The requirement for the Senate was nine years.

In 1790 Congress passed the first federal law on naturalization. It allowed "free white" persons who had resided for two years in the United States to be eligible for citizenship. Five years later, Congress increased the residency requirement to five years.

By the standards of the time, the framers had a very generous idea of citizenship and American nationality. Naturalization was easier in the United States than in any other country in the world. American nationality was tied to support for the ideals of the new country. People who wanted to join the American future were welcome. Americans were united not by the inheritance of birth but by a pledge of allegiance to the young country.

Immigrants Build the Nation's Capital

Three immigrants contributed their talents to the building of a new national capital, Washington, D.C.

- **James Hoban** grew up in Dublin, Ireland, and came to the United States as a young man. In 1792 Hoban submitted the winning design for the White House, based on an old Irish manor house.

- **Benjamin Latrobe,** an English immigrant, came to the United States in 1796. Latrobe took over the design of the United States Capitol in 1803 and also completed the House of Representatives from the plans of Dr. William Thornton. He designed the basic rotunda connecting the two wings of the Capitol in which each house of Congress meets.

- **Pierre Charles L'Enfant,** born in France, volunteered for the American army during the Revolution. In 1789 Congress decided to build a new city as the federal capital. L'Enfant applied for the job of chief architect and won the post. His final plan consisted of wide avenues fanning out from central squares like the spokes of a wheel. President Washington approved the plan and construction began.

Hairdressers and others in the beauty trade were often immigrants. Being a European meant you knew the latest styles.

This new country was larger than the thirteen colonies that hugged the Atlantic coast. The western boundary of the United States was the Mississippi River. Benjamin Franklin realized how important this vast territory was for future immigration. "Strangers are welcome," he noted, "because there is room enough for them all, and therefore the old inhabitants are not jealous of them."

Congress decided to make this land available to everyone: immigrants and native-born alike. It passed a law in 1785 that called for land in the Northwest Territory (the future states of Ohio, Michigan, Illinois, Indiana, and Wisconsin) to be sold at public auction. Two years later the Northwest Ordinance allowed these territories to become states when they reached a population of 60,000. This gave the governments of the territories an incentive to attract enough settlers to reach that level. They sent recruiting agents overseas to persuade people to emigrate. The Ordinance also guaranteed the residents of the territories freedom of religion and trial by jury, and prohibited slavery. These rights and freedoms also served to attract immigrants.

NEW IMMIGRANTS

Open immigration attracted many skilled and talented people. Despite the Revolution, many still arrived from the British Isles. The most important English immigrant in these early years was Samuel Slater. Slater came in 1791 with the plans for a spinning mill. With financing from Rhode Island merchants, he set up a factory to spin thread in Pawtucket, Rhode Island. This was the start of the cloth factories that over time would dot the New England countryside. It marked the beginning of American industrial strength that would one day dominate the world.

Immigrants both Protestant and Catholic came from Ireland. A young immigrant in New Jersey wrote home in 1796, "You can live better than in Best Man's house in Ireland. . . . Dear Brother Come here without fail as you Can

English immigrant William Colgate started a business that is still going today.

work at your trade . . . you can get a shilling a yard for weaving anything. . . . Bring your loom."

In 1789 the French Revolution began. The nobility and upper-class citizens of French society fled the country. During the next fifteen years, France went through more stages of revolution, which put one side and then another in control. The United States served as a haven, or refuge, for those on the losing sides. The word *refugee* was used for the first time to describe these people.

The French immigrants added to the Catholic population of the United States, and their priests eased a shortage of Catholic clergy. They also contributed to the civilized quality of life in America. The great French chef Anthelme Brillat-Savarin arrived in Philadelphia in 1793 and introduced the cheese omelet. French music and dance teachers and French-language tutors became the rage among wealthy American households. Even the Iroquois tribe hired a French dancing master. French fashions became up-to-date styles of clothing.

Many French refugees returned home when the political climate changed, but others remained permanently. One who stayed was Pierre-Samuel du Pont de Nemours. He arrived in the United States in 1799 and three years later his son founded E.I. du Pont de Nemours and Company in Wilmington, Delaware, to make gunpowder. The Du Pont company became one of the world's great chemical manufacturers.

A slave revolt in the French Caribbean colony of Saint-Domingue (today's Haiti) brought French colonists and their slaves to the United States. Many settled in Philadelphia, where they printed a daily newspaper with the latest news from the island. Others went to Baltimore, Charleston, New York, and New Orleans. Among the immigrants from Saint-Domingue was the famous painter John James Audubon.

Different viewpoints about the growing numbers of French and Irish immigrants defined the beginning of American political parties. The Federalist Party, led by John Adams, favored greater restrictions on immigration. When Adams was president, Congress passed the Naturalization Act of 1798. This raised the time an immigrant needed to live in the United States to be eligible for citizenship to fourteen years. That same year the Aliens Act authorized the president to arrest or deport any alien whom he considered dangerous to the United States.

This print of Slater's Mill in Pawtucket, Rhode Island, is from 1815. The mill used water power to run the cloth-weaving machines.

Living Like an Indian Queen

Many letters home emphasized the material richness of America, which fascinated newcomers. Their accounts often encouraged friends and relatives to come to the booming new country. From Germantown, Pennsylvania, Alice Barlow wrote home:

Dear Mother:

I want to say we are all in good health, and hope this will find you so. . . . Tell my brother John I think he would do very well here; my husband can go out and catch a bucket of fish in a few minutes; and John brings as many apples as he can carry, when he comes from school; also cherries, grapes, and peaches. We get as much bread as we can all eat in a day for seven pence altho' it is now called dear [expensive]. Dear mother, I wish you were all as well off as we now are: there is no want of meat and drink here. . . . Tell little Adam, if he was here, he would get puddings and pies every day. Tell my old friends I shall be looking for them next spring; and also tell my brother John and sister Ann, if they were here, they would know nothing of poverty. I live like an Indian Queen. . . .

Your affectionate daughter,
Alice Barlow

These laws were unpopular, particularly among immigrant Americans, whose votes eventually helped Thomas Jefferson win the presidency in 1800. The year after Jefferson's inauguration, Congress restored the five-year residency requirement, which has remained in effect to the present time.

During his administration, Jefferson bought the Louisiana Territory, which doubled the size of the United States. This enormous land made a liberal immigration policy necessary. The United States needed more and more people to clear the land, plant crops, and populate its fast-growing country.

In Europe, the rise of Napoleon Bonaparte to power in France led to major wars. This kept immigration from Europe relatively low until 1815. The fighting disrupted communications and travel. The decreasing number of new immigrants led to greater Americanization among earlier immigrants. The use of foreign languages such Welsh, Dutch, Irish, and German declined or ended, except in a few areas. But after Napoleon's defeat in 1815, Europe was once more at peace, and the number of immigrants to the United States was about to climb.

John Jacob Astor came to America from Germany with some flutes to sell. He became the first millionaire in the country.

CHAPTER FOUR

AMERICA FEVER

In 1843 the Bohnung family left Barkausen, their small village in northwest Germany, bound for America. Ernest, who was then ten, remembered:

"We knew very well what we had [in Germany], namely six acres of good land, located by the river, and good enough to get by on. Nevertheless my Father was not satisfied, for life went on in an endless cycle of manure wagon, spinning wheel, pumpernickel, sour milk and boiled potatoes. What's more there were nine children in the family, five of them boys. If we stayed, they might be drafted in the next war, and be shot to death for the King and Fatherland. Father had been a soldier himself, and did not want that fate for his sons. So the thought of leaving remained in his head. . . .

"It so happened that Ernst Borges [a neighbor] . . . decided to emigrate with his young family. Father declared that his older son, Heinrich, who would soon be drafted, would join Borges. . . . This was the advance scout of our family, in a way, a reconnaissance patrol. We could rely on what they would report, and that would determine what the whole family would do. . . .

"We anxiously waited for the first reports to arrive. In August they came, and were favorable. They convinced my father. . . . At last, we kids shouted, 'Hooray, we are going to America!'"

The Bohnung family was part of a mass migration of people from northern and western Europe, called "America Fever." From 1820 to 1860, more than 6 million Europeans came to the United States. The total population of the United States in 1820 was less than 10 million, so the impact of these immigrants was enormous. In proportion to the population already there, it was the greatest time of immigration in the nation's history.

No form of ad attracted more immigrants than the personal letter. The experience of a real immigrant family member was treasured and often shared with others.

Many people caught America Fever by reading. Guidebooks to America became best-sellers. Franz Ennemoser, who wrote one, was pretty clear about what the emigrant needed most: "There are three things he must always keep in mind: money, money, and money. To be successful, he will need plenty of money."

The real-life experiences of those who had already gone to America were the most important sales pitch. Nothing could beat a letter sent home by a satisfied immigrant. Families who received these "America letters" read them over and over and shared them with neighbors. Sometimes the letters were printed in the local newspaper.

Margaret McCarthy wrote to her father in Ireland, "Any man or woman are fools that would not venture to come to this plentyful country where no man or woman ever hungered or ever will."

"This is a free land," a German immigrant wrote home. "No one gives orders to anybody here. One man is as good as another. No one takes off his hat to another as you have to do in Germany."

America Fever spread and fed on itself. Relatives who had already come to the United States paid for family members in the old country to follow them. Sometimes not only their relatives but also their friends and many others in their home village followed in their path to America. This process is known as chain migration, and it still is part of the immigration process today.

Packet ships promised definite dates of departure, thus helping to regularize the immigrant trade.

Immigration Numbers

Here are the total immigration numbers for these decades, and the four nations that sent the most people.

1821–1830
143,439 immigrants.
Top four: Ireland, England and Scotland, France, Germany.

1831–1840
599,125 immigrants.
Top four: Ireland, Germany, England and Scotland, France.

1841–1850
1,713,251 immigrants.
Top four: Ireland, Germany, England and Scotland, France

1851–1860
2,598,214 immigrants.
Top four: Germany, Ireland, England and Scotland, France.

FLEEING HUNGER AND WAR

The largest group of newcomers during this time was the Irish. Poverty in Ireland was so terrible that it was said that "generations of Irishmen have lived and died without ever tasting meat." Although Irish farms produced grain and pork, those were taken by their landlords as rent and exported. What the Irish peasants lived on were potatoes. Thus, in 1845, when the potato crop was attacked by a fungus and the crop destroyed, the Irish faced starvation. The time remembered as "the Great Hunger" had begun.

Nicholas Cummins, the magistrate of Cork, described the horrible sights he saw. "Six famished and ghastly skeletons, to all appearances dead, were huddled in a corner on some filthy straw," he wrote of the first house he visited. "I approached with horror, and found by a low moaning they were alive. . . . The same morning, the police opened a house . . . which was observed shut for many days, and two

Emigrant Ballads

As America Fever raged in parts of northern and western Europe, many songs that captured that desire became popular.

Here is one from Sweden:

*Brothers, we have far to go
Over the salt water,
And then there is America
On the other shore.
Chickens and other fowl
rain down,
Cooked well-done and what
is more,
Fly on the table
With knife and fork stuck
in their thigh.
Isn't it possible?
Oh dear yes, it's so delightful.
What a pity that America
What a pity that America
Lies so far away.*

One from Norway:

*And now farewell to all my folk
and parish,
For I am going to America,
To seek a happier life in the
New World.
There is no help for it,
I must cross the sea —
Life has become too hard here
for poor folk.*

One from Ireland:

*With me bundle on me
shoulder,
Faith! there's no man could
be bolder;
I'm lavin' dear old Ireland
without warnin'
For I lately took the notion,
For to cross the ocean,
And I'm off for Philadelphia
in the mornin'.*

frozen corpses were found, lying upon the mud floor, half devoured by rats." By 1850 Ireland had lost over 2.5 million people. More than a million had died and nearly another million had emigrated, most to the United States.

The Germans formed the second largest group of immigrants during this time. Some of the German immigrants were young single men looking for a new life; others came in family groups or even as whole villages of people together. Many were highly skilled. They took whatever they could carry and sold the rest.

A mother and her son search desperately for any potatoes that might still be edible.

Many Germans had tried to form a united Germany with a democratic government. In 1848 an unsuccessful revolution dashed the idealistic hopes of the young people who joined it. Many who had taken part in the struggle headed for America. "The 48ers," as they were called, brought to America their idealism and interest in politics. Carl Schurz, a 48er who went on to a have political career in the United States, recalled his hopes on setting out for America in 1851. "It is a new world, a free world, a world of great ideas and aims. In that world there is perhaps for me a new home."

Refugees from other European upheavals came to seek greater freedom in the United States. The failure of the Polish rebellion of 1831 brought exiles to New York. A small number of Greeks came here to escape their nation's struggle against Turkey. The failure of the 1848 revolutions in other countries sent French, Czechs, and Hungarians to the United States. Almost 25,000 Czechs came to the United States between 1850 and 1860. Like the Germans, many of these people were highly educated or skilled.

LEAVING HOME

The departure was always heart-wrenching. "A deafening wail resounds as the station-bell gives the signal of starting," wrote an observer of Irish leaving their home villages. "I have even seen gray-haired peasants so clutch and cling to the departing child at this last moment that only the utmost of three or four friends could tear them asunder."

Crossing the Atlantic usually took about thirty days but with bad weather could last twice as long. The immigrants had to bring all their needs aboard ship — including bedding, usually a sack filled with clean straw. They also had to supply their own food. Because there was no refrigeration in those days, it was necessary to bring foods that would keep — flour, sugar, dried fruit, tea, coffee, smoked meat, and rice. And they also had to bring kitchen utensils, such as spoons, teapots, plates, and tin cups for cooking.

Those immigrants who waited to buy their supplies at the port of departure were often shocked at the prices. Merchants realized that the immigrants were captive customers and cheated them. Many people lost their life savings buying the necessary supplies — savings that they had hoped would give them a good start in America.

The steamer trunk often held clothes and family heirlooms as well as food that immigrants felt they needed for the journey.

CROSSING THE ATLANTIC

The ocean voyage was an ordeal. Anna Schweizer, who left Switzerland with her husband and two children in 1820, described the cooking facilities aboard ship: "Because of the danger of fire, the kitchen was on the deck, firmly held in place. However, if through carelessness a fire should occur, the kitchen, fire and all, could quickly enough be tossed into the sea."

Life was not completely grim on an immigrant ship. These Norwegians danced as they crossed the Atlantic.

Angela Heck, who traveled from Germany in 1854, was terrified by a storm that she described in a letter home: "The ship was listing to one side and all the top planks started to break. We had to hold on as tight as we could to keep from falling out. . . . You couldn't lie down, stand up or sit. . . . The stairs were then closed off since water was coming into the ship from the deck above and the small trunks started floating around. Our cooking pot and spoon floated all around. . . . We repented our sins and we all prepared to die."

ARRIVAL

Excitement grew aboard ship as the immigrants approached their destination. New York was the favorite port of entry. Christopher Castanis, a fourteen-year-old refugee from Greece, remembered his first sight of it: "The fog lifted, and there burst upon our vision a scene like a fairy dream. America greeted us, arrayed in a gorgeous robe of snow. As New York emerged from the mists, we stared in silent wonder at the tall church spires rising above the sparkling roofs of many buildings."

No sooner were the immigrants off the boat when they were assaulted by "runners" who grabbed their luggage and took them to a boardinghouse. The boardinghouses paid the runners for passengers.

A young Irish immigrant of the 1840s was accosted by two runners at the same time. One took his clothes, and the other grabbed his toolbox. An observer wrote, "Each [represented] a different boarding house, and each insisted that the young Irish man . . . should go with him. . . . Not being able to oblige both gentlemen, he could oblige only one; and as the tools of the trade were more valuable than the clothes, he fol-

With a knapsack holding a change of clothes, this newcomer is ready to start his new life.

The new arrivals had to beware of people who would take advantage of them. Note the thief going through a woman's purse.

Memories of the Voyage

For many immigrants, the ocean voyage to America was seared
into their memories. Here are a few recollections:

Edwin Bottomley, England: "Soon after we got to
bed the ship began to roll very hard and the sea
and the wind began to roar as if it was bent on the
destruction of everything floating upon it. Betwixt
12 and 1 o'clock it was the worst it was so bad
that we could scarcely keep in bed. . . . The
luggage belonging to the passengers rolled about
and cans and pots were strewed about in all places
and the noise all made was beyond description.
There was screaming and praying in every corner
and the sailors cursing and the waves rolling all
over the deck all at one time. Amidst all the
turmoil the grim monster Death entered and took
away the life of a child."

Elise Dubach, Switzerland: "Eight sheds, called
kitchens, were assigned to the steerage. These
were on deck, sheltered from rain or snow by a
roof, but otherwise open on all sides to the
weather. . . . Fire was laid by the seaman in the
troughs, and . . . the passengers were summoned

to cook. Woe to the passenger who did not respond
immediately; for the coals died down, and there
would be no more fire until the next meal! Woe to
the passenger who spilled the water . . . for water
was rationed, and he could get no more!"

Anonymous Jewish girl, Germany: "My oldest
sister, Faiga . . . died that night. . . . As soon as
the officers found she was dead, they
immediately took her from us and my mother
never saw her again although she begged and
implored them to let her dress [Faiga] as becomes
one of our kind, but all her beseeching was in vain.
The officers and crew threw [Faiga] into the
ocean. . . . My youngest sister, Miriam Rose, who
was 11 years old, died the next day about
sunset. . . . I noticed [her] closing her eyes and
she was no more. . . . I can see everything now as
then after more than 75 years. [Her sister's body
was thrown overboard.] The splash I shall never
forget if I live to be 100."

lowed in the path of the gentleman who had secured that portion of
the 'plunder.'" There were worse things that could happen. Some immigrants had their money or possessions stolen by swindlers and thieves.

New York State decided to open an immigration station to help
the immigrants avoid runners and other con artists. In 1855 Castle
Garden opened its doors as the official landing place for New York
State. Between that year and 1890 about 8 million immigrants
were processed at Castle Garden — about two out of every three
immigrants who came to the United States. Second only to New York
as an immigrant landing place was the city of New Orleans. Other
major ports of entry were Boston, Philadelphia, and Baltimore.

GOING TO WORK

Patrick Bryant had his own business in the 1830s. The oyster stand was a popular fast food feature of New York.

Many immigrants never ventured beyond the cities where they landed. The poorer ones worked as day laborers, loading and unloading ships, and hauling goods as cart men and porters within the city. They carried bricks and cemented them into place. Their work was not only backbreaking and unpleasant but paid very little. An Irish worker remembered waking up "before the Stars and working till darkness."

There was fierce competition for jobs in construction gangs and on the docks. Men roamed the streets of the cities looking for an opportunity. The work was often temporary and seasonal, meaning that it couldn't be counted on to support a family. Employers commonly withheld part of the workers' pay until the projects were finished. "Where they want labour, they will engage Paddy as they would a drayhorse," an Irish visitor reported.

TRANSPORTATION AND MINING WORK

These immigrants built the nation's early roads, canals, and railroads. The Erie Canal, which connected the cities of Albany and Buffalo, New York, opened in 1825. The canal enabled ships to travel from New York harbor into the Great Lakes, carrying cargoes and passengers to Cleveland, Chicago, and Detroit. With only their shovels and strong backs, hardy

Right: Irish women often worked in private homes where their lace-making skills were useful.

Andrew Carnegie's First Job

Andrew Carnegie came to the United States from Scotland in 1848 when he was thirteen. Fifty-three years later, he sold the steel company he had founded for four hundred and fifty million dollars. In his autobiography Carnegie described his early working experiences in Pittsburgh, where his family settled:

"My father found it necessary to give up hand-loom weaving and to enter the cotton factory of Mr. Blackstock, an old Scotsman in Allegheny City, where we lived. In this factory he also obtained for me a position as bobbin boy, and my first work was done there at one dollar and twenty cents per week. It was a hard life. In the winter father and I had to rise and breakfast in the darkness, reach the factory before it was daylight, and, with a short interval for lunch, work till after dark. The hours hung heavily upon me and in the work itself I took no pleasure; but the cloud had a silver lining, as it gave me the feeling that I was doing something for my world — our family. I have made millions since, but none of those millions gave me such happiness as my first week's earnings. I was now a helper of the family, a breadwinner, and no longer a total charge upon my parents. . . .

"Soon after this Mr. John Hay, a fellow Scotch manufacturer of bobbins in Allegheny City, needed a boy, and asked whether I would not go into his service. I went, and received two dollars per week; but at first the work was even more irksome than the factory. I had to run a small steam-engine and to fire the boiler in the cellar of the bobbin factory. It was too much for me. I found myself night after night, sitting up in bed trying the steam gauges, fearing at one time that the steam was too low and that the workers above would complain that they had not power enough, and at another time that the steam was too high and that the boiler might burst. . . .

"One day . . . Mr. Hay had to make out some bills. He had no clerk, and was himself a poor penman. He asked me what kind of hand [handwriting] I could write, and gave me some writing to do. The result pleased him, and he found it convenient thereafter to let me make out his bills. I was also good at figures; and he soon found it to be in his interest — and besides, dear old man, I believe he was moved by good feeling toward the white-haired boy, for he had a kind heart and was Scotch and wished to relieve me from the engine. . . ."

Irishmen dug the "Big Ditch," as it was called, often standing knee-deep in water and mud with mosquitoes torturing them.

A farmer watching other Irish immigrants labor on the National Road in Pennsylvania described them as the "immortal Irish brigade, a thousand strong, with their carts, wheelbarrows, shovels and blasting tools, grading the commons, and climbing the mountainside . . . leaving behind them a roadway good enough for an emperor to travel over."

Immigrants toiled in the nation's mines as well. Many immigrants from Wales and Cornwall had worked in the mines in Britain. Other miners came from Germany, such as Peter Klein, who settled in Pottsville, Pennsylvania. He wrote home that American miners dug twice as much as those in Germany. "Then you should know that they have coal here [deposits under the earth] that is from 4 feet up to 20 and 30 and 40 feet high. That's to let you know there's only a handful of coal in Germany, compared to here." Irish, too, toiled in the mines digging the "bloody coal."

WOMEN AND CHILDREN'S WORK

Immigrant women worked as domestic servants in the homes of the wealthy and the middle class. Irish immigrant women often arrived without family or husbands, and eagerly accepted live-in servant jobs that offered free room and board. Irish families often sent their daughters to America first, because it was easier for them to save money to bring over the rest of the family. So many Irish women worked in domestic service that the Irish name "Norah" was used for any female houseworker.

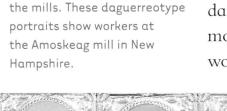

Immigrants often worked in the mills. These daguerreotype portraits show workers at the Amoskeag mill in New Hampshire.

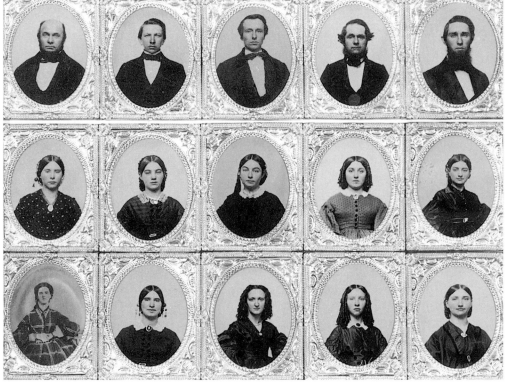

Scandinavian and German immigrant women also went into domestic service. The pay was much higher than for the same work in Europe. Marie Klinger, a German who emigrated in 1849, told her family that she made in one month what she would have been paid for a year's work in Germany. An 1853 Swedish guidebook to America assured its readers that "foreign serving

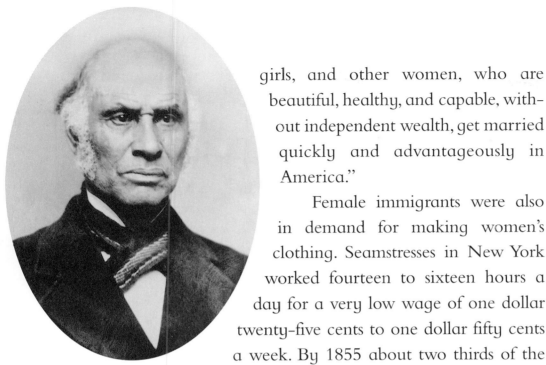

Antoine DeSant from Cape Verde, an island off Africa, was a New England whaling captain.

girls, and other women, who are beautiful, healthy, and capable, without independent wealth, get married quickly and advantageously in America."

Female immigrants were also in demand for making women's clothing. Seamstresses in New York worked fourteen to sixteen hours a day for a very low wage of one dollar twenty-five cents to one dollar fifty cents a week. By 1855 about two thirds of the New York dressmakers, hatmakers, seamstresses, embroiderers, and makers of artificial flowers were immigrant women. Some women were able to open their own businesses in these fields.

Children found jobs, too. Some worked as food vendors, selling such popular items as oysters, hot corn, sweet potatoes, tea cakes, and baked pears. Others shined shoes and sold newspapers. Working in stables taking care of horses, or even just holding a horse-drawn cart while the driver made a delivery, were jobs children could do. Recycling was a way of life in that era, and many children collected rags and paper for resale; some even combed the dumps for things of value.

The expanding textile mills of New England needed workers to tend the machines. In 1836 less than 4 percent of the women operators were foreign-born. By 1860 the figure was over 60 percent. It was hard work, with long hours and low pay, but it was the best that Irish women could find. Despite the hazards, poor working conditions, and low pay, the mills became a starting workplace for many different immigrant groups in the decades that followed.

A Peddler's Tale

William Frank, a German Jew, arrived in New York in 1840. He took up peddling — a route to riches that sometimes led to a country store and then perhaps a department store. Frank described how he got started:

"Here again I had a cousin living by the name of Frank. I hunted him up and remained with him overnight, He loaned me $3 with which to reach Philadelphia, where my stepbrother, Phillip Frank, lived. He was a shoemaker and had several journeymen working for him. He had a nice business but was a poor manager, and his wife could spend more than three men could earn. He had made his start by peddling merchandise and had about four dollars' worth of odds and ends in a handkerchief, which he gave me to sell. I remained in Philadelphia seven weeks and purchased additional goods each day.

"During the three weeks I made the acquaintance [of] and purchased goods from Blum & Simpson, who gave me credit for goods to the extent of $100 to go peddling out of the city. I peddled in Lancaster County one year and sent my parents $700, for them and my sister Babet and brother Moses to come to America with. They came, but my sainted mother lived only six months after arrival."

The immigrants transformed the cities where they settled. New York City doubled in population in just the ten years between 1830 and 1840; much of the increase was due to immigration. By 1860 New York had more Irish inhabitants than any city in Ireland.

As the city grew, wealthy citizens moved away from the business area near the docks. Their homes were broken up into many individual rooms so that as many people as possible could be squeezed in. There was no incentive for landlords to keep the buildings clean, because the demand for apartments was so great. The squalid, crowded housing became home to many poor immigrants.

This daguerreotype shows a mother and daughter who came from Wales and worked in the mills of New England.

IMMIGRANT COMMUNITIES

In Boston, the Irish who came in the 1840s lived in shanties of their own making. Each was "a crude shelter, generally half board, half dug-out . . . without windows." They were thrown together with little thought that they would last. When a family could afford to move, they just abandoned their shanty for better housing. The abandoned shelter soon became home to newer arrivals.

Germans — many of them more skilled and hence more prosperous than the Irish — lived in *Kleindeutschlands* or "Little Germanys." Here *biergartens* (beer gardens) served German food and drink for the whole family, offering German bands and dancing as well. Poorer Germans lived in such areas as "ragpickers paradise, a row of wooden tenements which smelled of [the] putrefying flesh of bone boiling places and filthy rags in the cellars and sheds. People were overcrowded and overrun with dead animals and an assortment of dogs. In the winter, it was the children's task to find the rags, and shreds of paper beneath the snow. The sale of these materials brought a bare survival."

Immigrants formed organizations for socializing and self-protection. German 48ers brought a love of political arguments, singing societies, and *turnvereine,* athletic clubs that featured physical exercise and gymnastics. Their clubs sprang up in cities with large German populations such as New York, Baltimore, and Philadelphia. Turnvereine gym equipment and exercises influenced the physical education classes that later would be part of school programs. In 1843 German Jews founded B'nai B'rith, the first national Jewish fraternal organization.

RELIGION AND PREJUDICE

Immigration had an influence on American religions. The Irish and German immigrants produced an enormous increase in the Roman Catholic population. The Irish started to replace the French as the leaders of the American Catholic Church. German Jews Americanized their religion, making English the language for many prayers and dropping some of the Orthodox practices.

Even Protestant immigrants, as many Germans were, practiced their religion differently than the Congregationalists of New England. American-born Protestants were continually shocked by the way these new immigrants observed the Sabbath. The Germans

The Five Points was the worst slum in New York. It was home to many Irish immigrants.

Where Mrs. Lincoln Shopped

Alexander Stewart, who became the nation's second-wealthiest man, arrived in New York City in 1823 with some lace he had bought in Ireland. He opened a store and soon attracted customers. Stewart specialized in "dry goods"— cloth that women purchased to make clothes for themselves and their families.

Stewart realized that his customers visited many other shops to purchase all the items that made up a fashionable outfit. Besides cloth, they had to buy ribbon, buttons, accessories such as umbrellas, hats, and handbags, as well as corsets and other undergarments. In 1846 he opened his Marble Dry-Goods Palace where all these things were on sale. The store also employed seamstresses who would make clothing to order from a customer's purchases. This was the first department store, and it was a huge success. Mrs. Lincoln shopped there, as did most other fashionable women.

During the Civil War, Stewart took orders from the government for uniforms, a project that made him more than 2 million dollars a year. At his death in 1876, he had a fortune of about 40 million dollars.

Immigrants created their own social organizations. This certificate is for a German group, the Sons of Hermann.

Signs like this one were visible forms of the prejudice that Irish immigrants often endured.

saw Sunday as a day of rest — and fun. After church they liked to relax with friends in the traditional German biergarten, going on picnics, and even dancing.

Religious prejudice erupted in the 1830s with outbreaks of anti-Catholicism. Native-born Americans, primarily Protestants, accused the Catholic Church of trying to change American values. The Irish were the prime targets of prejudice. Their sheer numbers, their poverty, and their Catholicism offended many Protestants. It was common to see the phrase "No Irish Need Apply" in advertisements for jobs.

NATIVISM

There were political reasons behind the anti-immigrant movement. Immigrants had started to play an important part in American elections, often voting for Democratic candidates over the opposition Whigs. President Andrew Jackson, a Democrat, stood for the issues of the common man, and he became a hero to new voters.

In the 1850s, the prejudice against foreigners — called "Nativism" — led to the formation of the American Party. It called for requiring an immigrant to live here for twenty years before being eligible to become a citizen. The American Party advised its members not to vote for any Catholic. "America for Americans" was one of its slogans. Party members were commonly

A Fight with the Know-Nothings

Elise Dubach came with her family from Switzerland in 1855 when she was twelve years old. She described how she and her eight-year-old brother were victims of the prejudice of the Know-Nothings in Saint Joseph, Missouri. Because she and her brother spoke German, the other children thought they were "Dutch," a term for German immigrants, who called themselves *deutsch*.

"As I walked to school, I was taunted by 'Know-Nothing' children for being Dutch. To them all foreigners were Dutch [really German] or Irish; and while they did not know my nationality, they knew I was not Irish. Of course it annoyed me to be called Dutch, but their mocking tones annoyed me more. When I reported their taunts to Uncle, he told me not to care but to answer that Dutch was better than they. Next day a big boy ran after me, yelling:

"'Yaah, see the Dutch girl!'

"When he paused for breath, I retorted:

"'Dutch is better than you!'

"That surprised him and quieted him and it also gave me satisfaction.

"My brother Adolph did not fare so well. One day, the boardinghouse [where they were living] pump being out of order, Aunt Christine sent him to the public pump to bring a pail of water. A group of 'Know-Nothing' boys told him that no Dutch boy could draw water at that well. They threw him into the mud, spilled the water on him, soiled his clothing, and beat and kicked him; and as he ran crying toward home, they yelled after him:

"'Bawl, you Dutchman, you!'

"Adolph arrived home so disheveled and mud-splattered that I scarcely recognized him. His yellow curls were black with mud; his clothing was torn; his face was livid with bruises. Taking him into the house, I helped him wash himself. Father knew only the mountaineer's form of redress, which he promptly put into execution. Leading Adolph by the hand, he went to the public well, where Adolph pointed out the ringleader of the juvenile 'Know-Nothings.' Father seized and spanked the lad, who howled for help, while his comrades scattered.

"Either the howls or the reports of fellow gangsters reached the ears of the victim's mother, for the spanking was scarcely administered before she came running with a constable. Father was taken before a justice, who delivered a lecture in English, which Father did not understand, and fined him five dollars, which he did understand. I believe, however, that the spanking had a beneficial effect, for after that we were tormented less."

called the "Know-Nothings" because they were sworn to secrecy; when asked questions, they often would answer they "knew nothing." In 1854 and 1855, the Know-Nothings won some victories in New England and the border states. The next year, they ran former President Millard Fillmore as their candidate for president. He lost but the party won the governorship of Massachusetts and many state offices.

CHAPTER FIVE

FROM SEA TO SEA

In 1851 twelve-year-old Anna Howard traveled with her mother, two sisters, and a brother to their new home in northern Michigan. They traveled by railroad to Grand Rapids, where they met her older brother James. He had a horse-drawn wagon to take them to their new home. As Anna recalled:

"For us children the expedition took on the character of a high adventure. We . . . all had an idea that we were going to a farm. My mother's mental picture was, naturally, of an English farm. Possibly she had visions of red barns and deep meadows, sunny skies and daisies. What we found awaiting us were the four walls and the roof of a good-sized log house, standing in a small cleared strip of wilderness. Its doors and windows were . . . square holes, its floor also a thing of the future, its whole effect achingly forlorn and desolate.

"It was late afternoon when we drove up to the opening that was its front entrance, and I shall never forget the look my mother turned upon the place Father had prepared for us. She buried her face in her hands and sat for hours without moving or speaking. We stood around her in a frightened group, talking to one another in whispers. Our little world had crumbled under our feet. Never before had we seen our mother give way to despair."

From 1815 to 1860, the United States extended its borders from the Atlantic to the Pacific Ocean. To many immigrants, the most alluring thing about America was the dream of owning their own farm — something that in Europe was nearly impossible. Sometimes the dream had a dark side, as in the case of Anna's mother. Public land sold at one dollar twenty-five cents an acre and was available to immigrants as well as the native-born. Many states and territories needed people, and their legislatures tried to encourage settlement by allowing people to settle on land and not pay for it until later.

This Chinese miner is panning for gold around 1851. The California Gold Rush brought the first large number of Chinese immigrants.

The completion of the Erie Canal made it easier to get to the Midwest. Taking a steamboat from New York to Albany cost from twenty-five to fifty cents. At Albany the immigrants could choose between a canal boat or a railroad trip to Buffalo on Lake Erie. The canal took seven to ten days and cost about a dollar and a half. The railroad was quicker — only thirty-six hours — but more expensive at five dollars a trip. At Buffalo, steamboats ran daily to cities and towns on the Great Lakes. This was the route taken by many who headed for Ohio, Indiana, Illinois, Michigan, Wisconsin, and Minnesota from 1815 to 1860.

Settlers going to Missouri usually came through New Orleans and up the Mississippi River by steamboat. An Irish immigrant commented: "St. Louis is quite a fine town but there are a great many foreigners in it."

This German immigrant boy is carrying buckets of beer to thirsty customers in Milwaukee, where German-American workers demanded beer on the job.

THE GERMAN TRIANGLE

The largest number of immigrants to the Midwest came from Germany. Three cities had so many Germans that they became known as the German Triangle. They were Milwaukee, Wisconsin; Saint Louis, Missouri; and the largest, Cincinnati, Ohio.

In Cincinnati the Germans played a major role from the start. A native of Heidelberg, Major David Ziegler was elected the first president of the village council. A German created the city's first waterworks, and another became its first industrialist and steamboat operator. With the start of German mass migration around 1820, Germans poured into Cincinnati because they knew they could expect a hearty welcome. Many built brick houses in a neighborhood that got the name Over-the-Rhine because people had to cross a canal to reach it from the business district. (The Rhine is a major river in Germany.)

By 1850 Cincinnati had five German newspapers. Laws were printed both in English and German, and the German language was taught in the schools. The city hosted festive *Sangerfests,* or singing competitions, which brought together German singing societies from such cities as Louisville, Kentucky, and Milwaukee, Wisconsin.

Germans were the largest ethnic group in Saint Louis. The German language, customs, and organizations were part of the city's life. It had an immigrant aid society for Germans as early as 1818. German Catholics, Lutherans, and Jews all built houses of worship and founded social clubs and other institutions.

Steamboats like the *Chippewa* carried immigrants to destinations on the Great Lakes.

MOVING TO ILLINOIS

Scandinavian immigrants to the Midwest were usually farmers looking for land. In 1837 Ole Rynning led a band of Norwegian settlers to Beaver Creek, south of Chicago. Later, Swedes and a sprinkling of Danes also settled in Illinois. As a Swedish immigrant wrote home, "God's blessing rests upon everyone who is willing to work."

But the large sizes of the farms could be a disadvantage. A person could walk for seven or eight hours and not see another house. Loneliness and isolation weighed heavily on the spirits of people who liked companionship and neighbors.

Father Frederic Baraga, Missionary of the Northwest Territories

Frederic Baraga was born in 1797 in Laibach, capital of today's Slovenia. Baraga was a gifted student who entered the priesthood feeling that he had a vocation to become a missionary among the Native Americans.

In 1831 he traveled to Cincinnati, the jumping-off place for the wilderness. The local bishop made him a pastor for Native American converts. After twenty-two years of preaching and ministering to his flock, Baraga himself was made a bishop.

His diocese was a far-flung area of isolated villages and forts, extending beyond the borders of the United States. It included the upper peninsula and part of the lower peninsula of Michigan, northern Wisconsin, eastern Minnesota, and parts of Ontario, Canada.

Baraga spent much time traveling on snowshoes and in canoes. Once he walked on snowshoes for twenty-four hours without resting in bitter cold through deep snow with a heavy pack on his back and nothing to eat but a frozen piece of cake. As part of his work, he learned Native American languages and published books about them. The Ojibway grammar book and dictionary he compiled was the first standard work on that language.

LIFE IN MICHIGAN

Canadians have been coming across the border throughout United States history. Laura and Charles Haviland moved to a Quaker settlement in the Michigan Territory. Here they founded Michigan's first anti-slavery society and opened a small school at their farm. The Raisin River Institute opened its doors to boys and girls, blacks and whites.

Dutch settlers often made the trip to America as entire communities. Many members of the Dutch Reformed Church were unhappy with the practices of the state-sponsored church. Separatist clergymen like Christian van Raalte led followers to the Midwest. Van Raalte founded Holland, Michigan, in 1846.

Dutch-born Cornelia Schaddelee arrived in Michigan in 1847. She was shocked at the primitive nature of the settlement. "There we stood," she wrote, "on the shore of Lake Michigan, 4500 miles away from the mother-land, with no covering over our heads than the blue sky. . . . All that was to be seen was a few booths, constructed of sticks driven into the ground, and branches of trees overhead, in which a few families lodged for the time being. . . ."

Living conditions outside the cities were often primitive. Anna Howard Shaw remembered that there was no school within ten miles of her family's farm. They had brought a box of books, which were the only ones in that part of the country. A newspaper from the East was passed around and then used as wallpaper where it was read all over again. Because Anna's father liked to read aloud, they soon had visitors. People came from as far away as ten miles and stayed overnight to listen to him reading.

ATTRACTING IMMIGRANTS

Until 1836 Wisconsin was part of Michigan. When it became a separate territory, it made great efforts to attract immigrants. In 1841 Gustaf Unionus led a group of fellow Swedes to Pine Lake,

Wisconsin. The natural beauty of the location reminded him of Sweden.

Louis Bruemmer, a Czech immigrant, arrived as a young boy in 1854. He remembered that life was hard. It was the depth of winter, and his feet were frozen. Although he was only fourteen he "was expected to earn the pork and bread for the family; he made shingles while his feet were healing, and after being able to walk, loaded 2000 shingles on a hand sled to Michicott, three miles distant, to trade for flour and pork." The early Czech pioneers often made wooden shingles to barter for goods in towns, sometimes as far as twenty to thirty miles away.

Minnesota also advertised heavily for immigrants. Alexander Harkin and his recent bride, Janet, were immigrants from Scotland. He wrote about the journey to Minnesota Territory: "Suddenly, our driver told us that we were nearing the first settler's house. Janet and I instantly leaned forward, eager to catch sight of it. 'Sit back! Sit back!' the driver said. 'You won't be able to see it until we get closer.' Then in a few minutes, he pointed with his whip and said, 'There's the house over there.' We looked in the direction he pointed, but saw only what we supposed was a muskrat house by the edge of a small pond. Looking more closely, we noticed that there was something strange about this muskrat house — it seemed to have a door in the side of it. And then a stranger — not a muskrat, but a man — jumped out the door, smiling and waving at us. Here was our first Minnesota settler!"

German immigrants brought a great love of music with them. This children's band is entertaining passers-by in St. Louis.

In the 1820s and 1830s, many immigrants went to Texas, then a Mexican territory. Among them were Robert Kleberg and his family, who came to Texas in 1834 from Germany. His daughter Rosa, then a young married woman, described her arrival: "As we were carrying our baggage into the house, an Indian carrying two big hams on his back approached me, saying, 'Swap! Swap!' I retreated behind a table upon which lay a loaf of bread, whereupon the Indians threw down the hams, picked up the bread, and walked off. The Indians were in the main quite friendly. They were constantly wishing to exchange skins for pots and other utensils."

James McBride, a sea captain, and his family settled in Texas before it joined the Union.

Texas's growing Anglo population put the territory on a collision course with Mexico. In 1835 Texans set up their own government and captured the Mexican-held city of San Antonio. Further battles turned the tide of victory, and Texas gained its independence. Many immigrants fought in the Texan war of independence; they also helped write the constitution for the new republic.

ATTRACTIONS OF TEXAS

Texas was a republic for ten years, then in 1845 became part of the United States. Both as a republic and as a state, it sought more immigrants. In 1845 Prince Carl of Solms-Braunfels acquired land and founded the German settlement of New Braunfels. The next year, another German community was founded at Fredericksburg. The Germans were so numerous that by 1847 the Texas legislature agreed to publish all laws in German as well as English.

In 1854 Silesian Polish peasants arrived in Galveston, then the port of entry for Texas immigrants. They had learned about Texas through enthusiastic letters from a Polish priest named Leopold Moczygemba.

But when Polish immigrants arrived they saw nothing but sagebrush and rattlesnakes. Some of the 800 immigrants threatened to hang the good priest from the nearest tree, feeling that his letters had lied. But the next year they built a Polish Catholic church in the settlement of Panna Maria. Soon there were other Polish-Texan towns with names like Czestochowa, Kosciusko, and Polonia.

Life in Texas for immigrants could be very good. Augustin Haidusek, a Czech immigrant from the Austrian Empire, described the pride of his father in the farm he worked: "When four years [after our arrival] new immigrants came, some of them expressed surprise at the buildings we were living in. Several families stopped with us, among them Valentin Galia, a classmate of my father.

"After he looked at our building which was fairly good, he said, 'My dear Valento, you had a better pigsty at home.'

"My father answered, 'I had rather live in this hut as an American citizen than to live in a palace and be under the Austro-Hungarian oppression.'"

Arthur Szyk painted the construction of the church
in the Polish Texan settlement of Panna Maria.

"We often held an umbrella over our bed. . . ."

Caroline von Hinueber was a young girl of eleven when she came to Texas from Germany in 1831. Her father, Frederick Ernst, was one of the earliest Germans to join the Austin colony. She described the early years:

"We moved into our own house. It was roofed with straw and had six sides, which were made out of moss. The roof was by no means waterproof, and we often held an umbrella over our bed when it rained at night, while the cows came and ate the moss. Of course we suffered a great deal in the winter. My father had tried to build a chimney and fireplace out of logs and clay, but we were afraid to light a fire because of our straw roof. So we had to shiver. Our shoes gave out, and we had to go barefoot in winter, for we did not know how to make moccasins. Our supply of clothes was also insufficient, and we had no spinning wheel, nor did we know how to spin and weave like the Americans. It was 28 miles to San Felipe de Austin, and besides, we had no money. When we could buy things, my first calico dress cost 50 cents per yard."

War with Mexico between 1846 and 1848 brought new territory and new citizens to the United States. The United States gained almost half the territory of Mexico. This included all of California, Nevada, Utah, and parts of New Mexico, Arizona, Colorado, and Texas. There were over 80,000 Mexicans already living in this immense area. They were given the right to stay and become United States citizens. In reality, they became second-class citizens, victims of prejudice that shunted most of them into barrios, where they kept their traditions alive.

IMMIGRANTS TO UTAH

A larger number of immigrants went west to Utah, a refuge for members of The Church of Jesus Christ of Latter Day Saints, called the Mormons. The Mormon Church was an American religion founded in New York State by Joseph Smith. He and his followers moved to Illinois, where Smith was killed by a mob. Fleeing persecution, the Mormons traveled west under the leadership of Brigham Young, finally settling in what became known as Salt Lake City.

Eager to attract converts to the church, missionaries went overseas. They were very successful in the Scandinavian countries, England, Wales, and Switzerland. The highly organized Mormons made travel arrangements for their immigrant converts. They reserved ship tickets, made train reservations, and blazed a trail all the way to Utah.

Priscilla Merriman Evans converted to Mormonism in Wales when she was seventeen. After she married an elder of the church, they traveled to Iowa City, where the couple joined Captain Bunker's Third Handcart Party, a group of 3,000 Mormons walking to Utah while dragging handcarts with their belongings behind them.

Evans remembered the 1,330-mile trek: "There were a great many who made fun of us as we walked, pulling our carts, but the weather was fine and the roads were excellent and although I was [pregnant]

This Jewish immigrant, who came to Oregon in 1857, poses with a knife and pistol to impress his family back home.

The First Woman to Climb Pike's Peak

Julia Archibald Holmes was born in Nova Scotia in 1838. Her family emigrated to the United States and settled in Kansas. After marrying James Holmes, Julia went with him to Colorado looking for gold. On that trip, when she was twenty, Julia became the first woman to climb Pike's Peak. She proudly wore the bloomers [resembling Turkish pants] that identified her as an advocate of women's rights. She wrote a letter to her mother from the top of the mountain:

Dear Mother,
I have accomplished the task which I marked out for myself, and now I feel amply repaid for all my toil and fatigue. Nearly everyone tried to discourage me from attempting it, but I believed that I should succeed; and now here I am, and I feel that I would not have missed this glorious sight for anything at all. In all probability I am the first woman who has ever stood upon the summit of this mountain and gazed upon this wondrous scene, which my eyes now behold.

and we were tired out at night, we still thought, 'This is a glorious way to come to Zion.' . . . My husband, in walking from twenty to twenty-five miles per day [suffered] when the knee rested on the pad [as a young boy he had lost his left leg at the knee in an accident]. The friction caused it to gather and break and [become] most painful. But he had to endure it, or remain behind, as he was never asked to ride in a wagon. . . .

"We reached Salt Lake City on October 2, 1856, tired, weary, with bleeding feet, our clothing worn out and so weak, we were nearly starved, but thankful to our heavenly Father for bringing us to Zion."

Mormon immigrants moved to Salt Lake City in highly organized wagon trains. This party has reached Needles Rock in Utah.

In January 1848, gold was discovered at the sawmill on John Sutter's ranch on the Sacramento River. Sutter, a Swiss immigrant from Germany, hoped to keep the discovery secret, but word spread quickly.

The wealthy California Spanish known as Californios lived in prosperity and took great pride in their culture.

Ships stopping at San Francisco suddenly lost their crews — and often their officers, too — when they heard about the gold. Before long, the harbor was crowded with empty, abandoned ships. By the next year, a gold rush had brought people from all over the world, seeking their fortunes.

THE WORLD COMES RUSHING IN

Gold fever struck particularly hard in France. The French government encouraged people to go to California, and financial speculators paid for their trips in return for a share of the profits. There was even a French newspaper devoted entirely to stories about the discoveries of gold being made. By 1853 there were 30,000 French in California.

People came from closer countries, such as Canada, Mexico, and the nations of South America. Latin Americans, particularly those from Mexico and Chile, encountered prejudice from the white prospectors. Some were brutally attacked and forced out.

In 1848 there were just fifty-four Asians in California. One was a San Francisco merchant named Chum Ming. He wrote to a friend in China about the gold rush. News also spread to China from ships arriving in Canton harbor. Circulars giving optimistic views of what the United States was like were passed through southern China. One read, "Americans are very rich people. They want the Chinaman to come and will make him welcome. There will be big pay, large houses, and food and clothing of the finest description. . . . it is a nice country without mandarins [officials of the Chinese Empire] or soldiers. All alike; big man no larger than little man."

A Mexican Californio in the Gold Rush

Antonio Franco Coronel was born in Mexico and came to California with his father in 1834, when he was sixteen. The ranch they started was later taken from them by a U.S. Land Commission after California became a state. Even so, he became mayor of Los Angeles in 1853, and served in other state offices. He kept a journal in which he described his adventures during the Gold Rush. Here he relates what he saw on first arriving in the gold fields:

"In the gold field there was quite a population of Chileans, Peruvians, Californians, Mexicans, and many Americans, Germans, etc. The campsites were almost separated by nationality. All — some more, some less — were profiting from the fruits of their labor. But then the news went around of the expulsion from the mines of all those who were not American citizens, because it was felt that foreigners did not have the right to exploit the mines. . . .

"There were a considerable number of people of various nationalities to whom this order to leave applied. They decided to gather on a hill in order to be on the defense in case of attack. The day on which the departure of the foreigners was supposed to take place, and during the next three or four days, both forces remained cautious, but the event did not go beyond shouts, gunshots, and drunkenness, and finally everything calmed down and we returned to continue our work, although daily some of the weak were despoiled of their claims by the stronger."

To peasants working in the rice paddies, images of *Gum San,* or Gold Mountain, seemed inviting. By 1850 there were more than 4,000 Chinese in California, and two years later 20,000 landed. The new arrivals, with their straw slippers and hair braided in a queue (pigtail), were at first objects of curiosity and then targets of prejudice. The majority were men intending to return home after making their fortunes.

Chinese men like this California miner wore a braid, or queue, at the command of the Chinese government.

THE MINING CAMPS

Most of the Gold Rush arrivals came through San Francisco. From there they traveled up the Sacramento River to the Sierra Mountains where the gold was. The miners often settled in camps of their own nationality. For example, there were French camps, German camps, and Chinese camps. As in the cities of the East, new immigrants felt most comfortable among their own people.

This Frenchman, M. Derbec, is shown with all the mining equipment he needs to make a strike—if he was lucky.

In the early days gold was easy to find in the streams. All a miner needed was a pan and rocker — a method learned from the Mexicans. Soon these were replaced by the sluice, a long wooden trough where gold flakes were separated from sand and dirt. Later, commercial mining technologies washed away parts of hills to find the gold that lay beneath.

A Norwegian miner wrote home, "The work is extremely hard. I start at 4 o'clock in the morning and keep on till 12 noon. After that I rest for three or four hours, for at that time of day, the heat is unbearable, and then I work again till 8 o'clock in the evening. The nights here are exceedingly cold. We live in tents; I have not been inside a house since April 1. The ground is our bed and a saddle or something like that our pillow."

HOW TO GET RICH

The surest way to get rich in the Gold Rush was to sell goods to the miners — both those who were arriving and those with gold in their pockets. Miners' wives often made more money than their husbands by doing laundry. The price of food, clothing, and other necessities skyrocketed. Russian-born Morris Schloss arrived with a peddler's wagon in a wooden crate. As soon as the crate had been unloaded from the ship, Schloss recalled that "a man asked me what was in the box. I told him, a wagon, and he asked the price of it. I answered $125, and he offered me $100. . . . I accepted his offer, and he paid me in gold dust. I had only paid $15 for this wagon in New York, so I thought this was rather a good beginning for me.

"The man . . . taking out the wagon . . . said to me: 'Stranger, you

A Frenchman Finds Work in San Francisco

A French immigrant, Montes Jean, wrote his father about how he and his companions survived after their arrival in California in 1849. They were not able to go to the gold-mining area because heavy rains had caused floods.

"We have been fortunate being in a country where a great deal is earned and where work is not lacking. I say 'work'; that is to say, go to the dock of San Francisco, become a working man, carry bales of merchandise to various stores, and you will be quite well paid. For carrying a trunk weighing about a hundred livres [pounds] for a distance of fifty meters or more one is paid three dollars (about sixteen francs) and in this way we have lived up to now."

may keep the wagon, for I only want the box . . . I am a cobbler, and in the daytime it will be my shop, and at night, my residence.' That box measured seven feet by four feet."

Many fortunes were made from selling supplies to the miners. One Bavarian Jewish immigrant, Levi Strauss, sold them pants made with strong cotton cloth and held together with rivets. That was the beginning of the Levi's blue jeans business. The first millionaire in California was Sam Brannan, who learned of the gold at Sutter's Mill and cornered the market for digging equipment, which he sold to the new arrivals.

The California Gold Rush set off the largest voluntary migration in world history. Within a year the non–Native American population jumped from 20,000 to 100,000, and the next year, 1850, California became a state. By 1854 California had 300,000 people, and San Francisco was the nation's sixth busiest port. Half of the city's population were immigrants. In contrast, one out of ten Americans overall were foreign-born. From then until the present day, California has continued to be a magnet for new Americans, second only to New York City.

Getting to California fast to strike it rich was the name of the game. It was often quicker to go by ship around Cape Horn than to cross the plains by wagon.

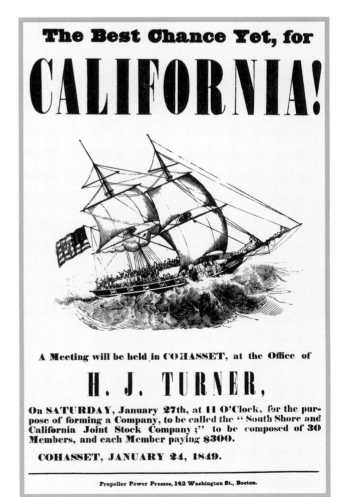

The Best Chance Yet, for

CALIFORNIA!

A Meeting will be held in COHASSET, at the Office of

H. J. TURNER,

On SATURDAY, January 27th, at 11 O'Clock, for the purpose of forming a Company, to be called the "South Shore and California Joint Stock Company;" to be composed of 30 Members, and each Member paying $300.

COHASSET, JANUARY 24, 1849.

Propeller Power Presses, 142 Washington St., Boston.

After the Civil War, free homesteads attracted many immigrants. This Norwegian family is taking a coffee break on the North Dakota prairie.

CHAPTER SIX

DIVISION AND REUNION

Thomas Hunt, an Irish immigrant, served in the Union Army
during the Civil War. In 1862 he wrote to his brother:

*"It is nothing but ruin in this part of the south. As far as the eye can see in
all directions it is one vast plane of ruin. This is or was a little while since
a beautyful country. I have seen some of Varginia and their is not a sign of
a fence in any part of that I have seen. The soldiers have used the rales for
fire and the board fences for many other purposes. . . .*

*"Many a poor fallow have I seen dead and dying on the field and in
a litter of straw in the barn yards. This has been a long line of battle. The
lines of strife ware visible in maney places by the dead bodeys of our soldiers
and them of our enemy. This is one vast burying ground."*

The Civil War was the nation's bloodiest war. The years from 1861 to 1865
were the greatest crisis and test of unity in our history. Because the greatest number of immigrants had settled in the North, they provided many more
soldiers for the Union side. But immigrants who lived in the South served the
Confederacy as well, even when they were personally opposed to slavery.

During the war Congress passed two acts that would have far-reaching
effects in the years that followed. The first was the Homestead Act of 1862, which
offered 160 acres of government land free to homesteaders who agreed to live on
it for five years. The other bill was the Pacific Railroad Act, which provided funds
to build a railroad that would link America from coast to coast for the first time.
With the help of immigrant laborers, mostly Irish and Chinese, it became a reality before the 1860s were over.

After the Union victory in the Civil War, the reunited nation experienced
a period of great industrial expansion. Factories hummed with increased productivity; new industries like steelmaking grew in size and power. This growth
was made possible in part by a huge number of new immigrants who came here
after the war.

When the fighting began in April 1861, enthusiasm ran high in both the North and the South. Volunteers rushed to sign up. Elise Dubach, a Swiss immigrant, had been married for just two weeks and wrote, "Even after Fort Sumter had been fired on, our friends, both northern and southern, predicted that the war would be a mere 'breakfast job.'"

Elise was soon to learn otherwise. The state of Missouri, where she was living, was bitterly divided. Some residents wanted the state to secede and join the Confederacy, others backed the Union. What turned the tide was the presence of large numbers of German immigrants in Missouri who opposed slavery. They flew the Stars and Stripes over their meeting halls and strongly backed President Lincoln and the Republican Party. German efforts kept Missouri in the Union.

Union Army Sergeant David Urbansky relaxed after fighting by reading a book. He won the Congressional Medal of Honor for his bravery.

IMMIGRANT SOLDIERS

Immigrants swelled the Union ranks. Army recruiting agents met arrivals at Castle Garden to offer them a cash bounty to sign up for military service. Many immediately enlisted. Other immigrants who had left home to avoid being drafted were less enthusiastic.

A newly arrived immigrant sometimes could earn more in the army than in civilian life. A farmhand in the Midwest, for example, earned ten dollars a month. But a soldier was paid thirteen dollars. Also, many immigrants

Who Was Coming

1861–1870

2,314,824 immigrants.
The Top Nations:
Germany — 787,468
United Kingdom —
606,896
Ireland — 435,778
Canada — 152,878

1871–1880

1,812,191 immigrants.
Germany — 718,182
United Kingdom —
548,043
Ireland — 436,871
Canada — 383,640

1881–1890

5,246,613 immigrants.
Germany — 1,452,970
United Kingdom —
807,357
Ireland — 655,482
Canada — 393,304
Sweden — 391,776

wanted to show their loyalty to their new country. Anna Howard Shaw, an English immigrant in Michigan, remembered: "When the news came that Fort Sumter had been fired on . . . our men were threshing. . . . I remember seeing a man ride up on horse back, shouting out Lincoln's demand for troops and explaining that a regiment was being formed at Big Rapids. Before he had finished, the men on the machine had leaped to the ground and rushed off to enlist. In ten minutes not one man was left in the field."

Eager to show their patriotism, many foreign-born Americans joined the army in groups that trained and fought together. The first volunteer regiment that entered the Union Army from Chicago, for example, was organized by a Bohemian immigrant. In New York, both the Irish and Germans formed their own brigades. The French fought on both sides. New Orleans, with its large French population, provided many soldiers for the Confederacy. Other groups who served together included Italians, Poles, Danes, Russians, and Hungarians. All these ethnic military units usually had special insignia and uniforms that showed their common origin.

Many Italians fought in the Civil War in the Garibaldi Guard. Garibaldi had been one of the leaders of the fight for Italian independence.

VALOR ON THE BATTLEFIELDS

Immigrants took part in the bloodiest battles of the war. The Irish Brigade under Thomas Francis Meagher fought at Bull Run wearing green twigs on their coats. Meagher led his men on to Antietam and Fredericksburg in 1862, where the vast majority of them were killed. Captain Michael O'Sullivan wrote home

Fighting at the Battle of Antietam

Samuel Bloomer emigrated from Switzerland and at twenty-five served with the First Minnesota Volunteer Infantry in the Civil War. He kept a diary and described his service at the battle of Antietam in 1862:

"Wednesday, Sept. 17. We were up very early. Got our coffee. It's about 7 o'clock. We fell in line, forded Antietam Creek marched about 1 mile, formed in line of battle & Advanced through fields, Woods & over fences & over the field where the Battle commenced early in the morning & which field was covered with dead & wounded of both sides. At last we halted at the edge of a cornfield by a rail fence, but still we were in the Woods. Had not been at the fence more than 15 minutes before the most terrific fire was pour[ed] into the left of our brigade from the rear to front & which fire came quickly down the line to the right where we were. The firing was [lively] for a time. But I never had to go to the rear for I was shot in my leg just below the knee. I had just got behind a large tree when the whole line was ordered to fall back which they did leaving me behind. . . . I was left on the field all day as the shot & shells of both armies playing in or about there all day cutting off limbs of trees & tearing up the ground all around me, & which made it a very dangerous place. But as luck would have it I got through safe. By that fence my partner Oscar Cornman was killed & one of Co. A. . . .

"Sept. 18th. During the night I slept considerable & was wake at daybreak by a noise at my head & found a Secesh [Southern soldier] pulling at my canteen stopper which he wish to take. Laid on the same spot all day. & my partner's dead body lay in my sight all the time. About 6 P.M. 4 Secesh came with stretcher & took me up to a barn where there were about 100 more of our men. . . . I for one slept but little last night for pain. During the night the Secesh skedaddled off for parts unknown to us. . . . The first man of our regt. that I saw was Cofflin of Co. I. Then Capt. Pelecan gave me some breakfast, & soon my dear cousin came to see me. About noon I was put in an ambulance & taken to Hoffman's barn Hospital & laid in the yard in the ground where I lay all night with most dreadful pain. There were in & around this barn some 5 or 600 wounded soldiers.

"Sept. 20th. This day will long be remembered by me for about 8 o'clock A.M. the Doctors put me on the table & amputated my right leg above my knee and from thence suffering commenced in earnest."

Despite his suffering, Sam Bloomer went home, married, and lived to the age of eighty-two.

after being wounded at Antietam, "We have fought the enemy and our brigade has been cut to pieces! Every man of my company has either been killed or wounded with the exception of eleven." Another member, Thomas Hunt, whose letter to his brother you read at the chapter opening, died at Gettysburg. His brother went to the battlefield to retrieve the body.

Jens Andersen, a Danish immigrant, wrote to a friend about the fierce fighting at Murfreesboro, Tennessee, in 1863: "We were shot at from three directions. Everyone began to flee, that is all of those who could flee; many already lay swimming in their own blood, and still many more would bite the dust that day. Our lieutenant colonel as well as many other brave officers and fine soldiers fell here. . . . It seemed like all the elements were in an uproar; fire, smoke and the thunder of the cannons, the explosion of bombs, the whine of the bullets and the screams of the wounded all combined to make the day horrible."

As the war dragged on, casualties mounted. The armies needed ever greater numbers of soldiers. More manpower was needed on the home front as well. In 1864 President Lincoln issued a call for immigrants to come to work in the North's factories and on farms. Federal agents went overseas to recruit laborers. The same year, Congress established a Bureau of Immigration to encourage the flow of immigrants.

In 1865 the North prevailed. For immigrants, the war had created strong feelings of patriotism and a sense of belonging to their adopted country. In the Civil War as in most other wars, fighting for the country transformed the immigrant into an American.

John Ericsson: Father of the Ironclad Ship

On March 9, 1862, thousands of people had lined up on both sides of the harbor at Newport News, Virginia. Those spectators were rewarded by seeing the first naval battle between ironclad ships, the Union's *Monitor* and the South's *Virginia*. Because the cannons of both ships were unable to pierce the armor of the other, the battle ended in a tie. But it marked the beginning of a new age in warfare.

The builder of the *Monitor* was John Ericsson, a Swedish immigrant who came to the United States in 1839. Before the *Monitor*'s success, he had tried to perfect an underwater propeller to replace the paddle wheels on steamships. Finally he succeeded. President John Tyler and a delegation of high officials and their wives came to watch the ship launching. A cannon accidentally exploded, killing the Secretaries of State and Navy and wounding many others. Ericsson was blamed.

Seventeen years later, the *Monitor* made Ericsson a national hero. He continued to work on futuristic projects like torpedoes and solar-powered engines until his death in 1889.

Some immigrants enlisted in the Union side right off the boat at Castle Garden. The bounty signs there were in English and German.

Construction of the transcontinental railroad had started even while the war was going on. But work began in earnest with the release of thousands of soldiers from the armies. The government awarded the building contracts to two companies. The Union Pacific would lay tracks going west from Omaha, Nebraska. The Central Pacific would start at Sacramento, California, and head east.

The Union Pacific hired Civil War veterans, freed slaves, Irish and German immigrants, and Native Americans. But the largest number of laborers were Irish. The work was backbreaking and dangerous. Frequently accidents happened when a rail fell on a man's foot or dynamite blasts went awry.

The Chinese built much of the railroad track in the Sierras. They constructed trestles like this one to support the tracks.

RACE TO PROMONTORY

The government paid each company according to the number of miles it laid. Both sides soon realized they were in a race. The Union Pacific workers got off to a quick start. Because they were building track on flatland, they could move swiftly.

Building east from Sacramento, the Central Pacific laborers soon reached the Sierra Nevada Mountains. Charles Crocker, one of the heads of the Central Pacific, began hiring Chinese workers. Eventually Chinese made up four fifths of the Central Pacific's workforce. Thousands came to build the "Smoke Dragon," their name for the railroad.

The Chinese were paid thirty dollars a month, fifteen dollars less than the Irish and other workers on the Union Pacific. They blasted tunnels straight through mountains rather than twisting around the

Chinese and Irish Workers Have a Dispute

Grenville Dodge, chief engineer for the Union Pacific, described the last stages of the railroad construction. Competition between the two railroads was so keen that after the two lines met, both sides continued to lay tracks. For the first time, this brought Chinese workers and Irish workers into contact with one another. Dodge recalled what happened:

"Between Ogden and Promontory each company graded a line, running side by side, and in some places one line was right above the other. The laborers upon the Central Pacific were Chinamen, while ours were Irishmen, and there was much ill feeling between them. Our Irishmen were in the habit of firing their blasts in the cuts without giving warning to the Chinamen on the Central Pacific working right above them. From this cause several Chinamen were severely hurt. Complaint was made to me from the Central Pacific people,

and I endeavored to have the contractors bring all hostilities to a close; but for some reason or other they failed to do so. One day the Chinamen, appreciating the situation, put in what is called a 'grave' on their work and, when the Irishmen right under them were all at work, let go their blast and buried several of our men. This brought about a truce at once. From that time the Irish laborers showed due respect for the Chinamen, and there was no further trouble."

high Sierras. After they reached the flats of Utah across the Great Basin Desert, the workers moved faster. They succeeded in laying ten miles of track in a single day — a feat that has never been equaled. On the last stretch, the race between the two railroads and their workers intensified. Finally, in May 1869, a grand ceremony at Promontory, Utah, celebrated the joining of the two railroads. A golden spike was hammered into the last piece of track.

Irish immigrants worked on the Union Pacific, coming from the east. They laid 680 miles of track before they reached the Rockies.

The Homestead Act of 1862 promised 160 acres to settlers willing to work and live on the land for five years. The newly built railroads made the Act even more effective. The railroad owners wanted settlers to come to the land the tracks had crossed — much of it in the prairie in the middle of the country. If people built farms and ranches there, they would use the railroad to send their products to market. Also, the railroad owners had received huge tracts of land from the government. That land would only be valuable if people settled there.

This group of Swedes had their picture taken on their arrival in Kansas, probably to send home to relatives.

Attracting Immigrants

The railroads did their best to attract immigrants. They issued pamphlets and ads and books that praised the wonders of what had earlier been called the Great American Desert. Some pamphlets were printed in more than ten languages. Recruiters offered discounts on ship fares and cheap land prices for those who wanted more than the 160 acres they got free. Some railroads even provided lodging for potential buyers to come and look at the land.

The promise of land was particularly attractive to Scandinavians and Germans. Low wages and crop failures pushed Swedes out of their homeland at the end of the 1860s. So massive was the emigration that it left some towns and villages half empty.

To attract Germans, North Dakota named its capital city Bismarck, after the statesman who unified Germany. German farmers were so highly regarded that the railroads even recruited those who lived in Russia. The Atchison, Topeka, and Santa Fe railroad agent had to dodge the Russian authorities, who didn't want the United States to take so many of their best farmers.

The Germans from Russia who settled on the plains from Kansas to North Dakota brought America a special gift: a hardy strain of wheat that could withstand the long, cold winters. For a time in the 1880s, Eureka, a small town in the Dakota Territory, became "the wheat capital of the world." Even today, this red emmer wheat makes the Great Plains one of the largest wheat-growing areas of the world.

Immigrants of many groups often cooperated to build a barn for neighbors.

THE PRAIRIE WAS A CHALLENGE

After all the promises about the lush lands, newcomers were often surprised and disappointed. The sea of grass in the middle of the country was vast and unfamiliar. Towns were few and far between, and the prairie could be a lonely, spooky place at night.

Anton Senger, a German from Russia, came to North Dakota as a

Christmas Mumming in the Dakotas

The Raaen family from Norway settled on the Dakota prairies in the 1880s. One of their girls, Kjersti, described the fun activities for the New Year celebrations. "Mumming" was a bit like our Halloween festivities.

"Aagot [her sister] dressed Tosten [her brother] and me. She put a long white dress of her own on him and tied a cord around his waist. She made a mask out of part of a flour sack. . . . There we made holes for the eyes and nose, charcoal marks for eyebrows, and a stiff paper rolled to look like a long nose. She cut an opening under the nose and sewed some red cloth on for lips; it was an awful-looking mouth, so crooked! After she put the mask on Tosten, she put Mor's old black hood on his head. Tosten was a witch.

"She fixed me up so they would think I was a boy dressed like a girl. She had Far's [father] old coat, cap, and mittens, Mor's old skirt, and Aagot's old shoes, so large they looked like boys' shoes. . . . She tied a red kerchief on my head. It was good that we had so many clothes on outside our own, for it was a cold night.

"We always have a good time at Even Midboe's, so we decided to go there; he lives about a mile from us, but we didn't mind the distance because we had so much fun on the way. . . . Before we knocked at the door, we decided that only Tosten should talk, because he can disguise his voice. Even must have heard something; he opened the door and saw us before we had a chance to knock. . . . It was so warm in his house that we thought we would melt. When the children saw Tosten they were scared and began to cry. . . .

"Even's wife, brought cookies, apples, and candy, and a glass of Christmas mead for each. We could not eat with our masks on; so we had to take them off. How surprised they were when they saw that the witch was Tosten!"

boy in 1886. He recalled his first night: "I was scared to death, and felt sure some unknown animal would surely eat us up during the night. . . . I didn't sleep a wink. There were millions of mosquitoes. Then every little while a coyote would howl on one side then a fox on another, and to make it more miserable for me, a night owl would let out a screech in between. All of those different noises kept the chill running up and down my back all night and I was glad when morning came."

Taming the prairie was a great challenge. The roots of the grasses were so densely intertwined that it was difficult to push a shovel through them. Bit by bit, the sod had to be cut up and ripped out. Frequently, the sod had snakes living in it that did not like being disturbed.

The hardy immigrants, however, found a use for the blocks of sod they removed: They used them to build houses. These sod houses were waterproof, and on the inside they could be whitewashed to make them attractive. There were some drawbacks. Over time, the sod would settle and the ceiling and walls could become lopsided. The inside of a sod house was usually damp as well. Worst of all, small animals, insects, and worms came along with the sod and shared their living quarters with the humans.

The weather was brutal. In the summer it was burning hot. The winter brought blizzards, with snow drifting higher than the tallest person. Ida Lindgren, a young Swedish woman who came to Kansas, wrote: "It was so cold, so cold, the week before Christmas. . . . We have a thermometer with us from Sweden which cannot show anything lower than twenty-five degrees, but it was below that; . . . Gustaf's watch, which was in his vest pocket in among his clothes, stopped one night from the cold. When Gustaf warmed it up again in the morning, it started to go again; it was terrible."

Most dreaded of all was the appearance of swarms of locusts that occurred several times in the 1870s. A Czech girl remembered a plague of locusts in Nebraska: "We heard a sound and it grew dark and we thought that a storm was coming. The sun was hidden. We thought that it was the end of the world. Then they began to come down. In one hour they had eaten everything. . . . They bent down little trees with their weight. They were so thick on the ground that when we took a step they were over our ankles and our feet made holes like footprints in the snow. The river was covered with them so that in some places we could not see

This Norwegian immigrant uses a hoe to cut through the tough grass and brush that covered the Great Plains.

A German immigrant family stands outside their sod house to pose for a picture. The family pig is larger than the younger children.

These Chinese firefighters won a competition in Deadwood, South Dakota, in 1888.

A schoolroom of Danish children in Clinton, Iowa, had a stuffed crane.

the water. They would eat the paint off a house and chew up lace curtains. Sometimes they were so thick on the rails that they stopped the trains. The masses of them in the river made a terrible smell afterward, but it did not seem to cause any sickness."

CHICAGO

Chicago became the largest city in the heart of the country. By 1890 it was the second largest in the entire United States. Its growth was tied to its role as a hub of the railroad systems between east and west.

Chicago was truly a melting pot for people of many nations. Germans and Irish had settled there since before the Civil War. The city had the largest Swedish population of any city except

An Immigrant in the Chicago Fire

A Russian Jewish immigrant named Morris Horowitz came to Chicago in 1870. More than sixty years later, he described the great fire of 1871 that almost destroyed the city:

"We were getting ready to go to bed, when we heard the fire bells ringing. I asked the two men [other roomers at his lodging] if they wanted to see where the fire was.

"'Why should I care as long as our house is not on fire,' one of the men said. 'There is a fire every Monday and Thursday in Chicago.' But I wanted to see the fire, so I went out into the street. I saw the flames across the river, but I thought that since the river was between the fire and our house, there was nothing to worry about. I went back to bed. The next thing I knew my two bedfellows were shaking me. 'Get Up!' they cried. 'The whole city is on fire! Save your things! We are going to Lincoln Park.'

"I jumped out of bed and pulled on my pants. Everybody in the house was trying to save as much as possible. I tied my clothes in a sheet. With my clothes under my arm and my pack on my back, I left the house with the rest of the family. Everybody was running north. People were carrying all kinds of crazy things. A woman was carrying a pot of soup, which was spilling all over her dress. People were carrying cats, dogs, and goats. In the great excitement people saved worthless things and left behind good things. I saw a woman carrying a big frame in which was framed her wedding veil and wreath. She said it would have been bad luck to leave it behind. . . .

"No one slept that night. People gathered on the streets and all kinds of reasons were given for the fire. I stood near a minister talking to a group of men. He said the fire was sent by God as a warning that the people were wicked. He said there were too many saloons in Chicago, too many houses of prostitution. A woman who heard this said that a fire started in a barn was a direct warning from God since Jesus was also born in a barn. I talked to a man who lived next door to Mrs. O'Leary, and he told me that the fire started in Mrs. O'Leary's barn."

Stockholm. Poles built their first Chicago parish around Saint Stanislaus Church in the 1860s. In the next decade, Polish immigrants flooded into Chicago, finding jobs in the city's factories. Skilled Czech laborers came next; by 1870 the Czech community of Chicago was the largest in the United States.

In Europe the ancestors of Chicago's immigrant groups had often gone to war against one another. In America they formed clubs that battled in gyms and playing fields. Like the German turnvereine, groups such as the Czech Sokols, Polish Falcons, and Scottish Caledonian clubs combined gymnastics with culture. All stressed physical fitness and fellowship. Daily exercise periods became part of both the grade-school and high-school programs, forerunners of today's physical education programs.

PROSPERITY AND POVERTY

In 1869 California created the Immigrant Union to encourage immigration from Europe and the eastern parts of the United States. Rebekah Kohut, the daughter of a rabbi who had moved to California, remembered: "The state of California was at its period of greatest romantic appeal. . . . The West allured with many tales of the land flowing with milk and honey."

The Neelys, an Irish family in Oregon, spend an evening making music and popping corn over the fire.

California's publicity posters emphasized the state's cheap and fertile land and its mild climate, which was claimed to promote health and wealth. In a slap at the prairie states, pamphlets and flyers emphasized that the state was "without cyclones and blizzards." The immigrants who arrived after the Civil War were no longer looking merely for gold but for the wealth they could themselves produce from the land.

RICHES OF THE GOLDEN STATE

California was on its way to becoming the nation's most important agricultural state. With the completion of the railroads, it could ship its produce anywhere in the country. Land was abundant and fertile. Some immigrants obtained large plots of land and started major agricultural businesses. The German immigrant Claude Spreckels gained the nickname "the Sugar King" because of his thousands of acres of sugar beets. Many immigrants from France, Italy, and Germany planted grapevines

Female immigrants from northern and central Europe provided household help for wealthy and middle-class families.

from their native lands and started making wine. The father of the California wine industry was Colonel Agoston Haraszthy, a Hungarian immigrant who planted the first vintage quality vines at his Buena Vista Ranch in the Sonoma Valley.

Serbs and Croatians played an important role in developing the fishing trade in the waters off San Francisco. As more of these southern Slavic people came to the San Joaquin Valley, they planted apple orchards and grape vineyards. Stephen Mitrovic was a pioneer who imported cuttings of Adriatic fig trees from his native land in today's Croatia and developed the harvesting and packing of figs.

California's most important source of agricultural labor after the Civil War was the Chinese immigrants. They grew the sugar beets for the Spreckels Sugar Company and cleared the land to plant the vines for Colonel Haraszthy. Some Chinese immigrants started their own

Fair Play in America

Michael Pupin was a young Serb from the village of Idvor in Austria-Hungary. He came to the United States in 1874 and describes his first experience:

"My first night under the Stars and Stripes was spent in Castle Garden. . . . Early morning saw me at my breakfast, enjoying a huge bowl of hot coffee and a big chunk of bread with some butter, supplied by the Castle Garden authorities at Uncle Sam's expense.

"Then I started out, eager to catch a glimpse of New York. . . . Suddenly I was surrounded by a crowd of boys, jeering and laughing and pointing at my red fez [a Turkish cap]. They were newsboys and bootblacks who appeared to be anxious to have some fun at my expense. I was embarrassed and provoked but controlled my Serbian temper.

"Presently one of the bigger fellows walked up to me and knocked the fez off my head. I punched him on the nose and then we clinched. My

wrestling experiences on the pasture lands of Idvor came to my rescue. The bully was down in a jiffy and his chums gave a loud cheer.

"Suddenly I felt a powerful hand pulling me up by the collar and when I looked up I saw a big official with a club in his hand. He looked decidedly unfriendly but, after listening to appeals of the newsboys and bootblacks who had witnessed the fight, he softened and handed me my fez. The boys, who a little while before had jeered and tried to guy me, had evidently appealed in my behalf when the policeman interfered.

"America was different from Austria-Hungary . . . I was in a country where even among the street urchins, there was a strong sentiment in favor of fair play, even to a Serbian greenhorn."

small farms. They pioneered in developing what later became known as "truck farms," growing crops that could be shipped to nearby markets. Chinese farmers selling cucumbers, tomatoes, beans, strawberries, and melons from wagons became a familiar sight in California.

MINING AND RANCHING

New discoveries of valuable metals brought immigrant miners. Butte, Montana, was the center of a huge copper mining area, and Marcus Daly, an Irish immigrant, owned one of the largest mines and became a millionaire. He offered good wages to Irish workers and Butte's "Little Dublin" became the largest Irish settlement between Chicago and California.

Conditions were not so good for the iron miners in Missouri. Rosa Cristoforo left Italy to join her husband in a mining camp there. She was appalled: "There were no trees and no grass — just some shacks made of boards and some railroad tracks."

The silver mines of Arizona and New Mexico drew laborers from Mexico. Some Mexican farmers made migrating back and forth a way of life. They would leave their homes and families

This Chinese family settled in Idaho. Some members adopted American dress and others kept to the traditional style.

after planting their crops, travel to the mines in the United States to earn money, and then return home at harvest time. In those days there were no restrictions about crossing the border between the two countries and no border patrol.

Mexicans also played an important part in ranching and sheepherding in the West. Cattle ranching in Texas and sheepherding in New Mexico had begun when these territories were part of Mexico. Mexican vaqueros and sheepherders taught their skills to Anglos. The Basques — people from the region between Spain and France — also entered sheepherding. Soon they became the most valued herders in the West.

PREJUDICE

Chinese immigrants in the West met with protests and sometimes violence. Some Americans feared that the Chinese laborers were taking away jobs by working for lower wages. Denis Kearney, an Irish immigrant, organized opposition to the Chinese workers in California. Huie Kin described what it was like: "There were long processions at night with big torchlights and lanterns carrying the slogan 'The Chinese Must Go.' . . . We were simply terrified; we kept indoors after dark

Dutch farmers in Texas make rice levees with their mule teams near the small town of Nederland, named for their homeland.

for fear of being shot in the back. Children spit upon us as we passed by and called us rats. However, there was one consolation; the people who employed us never turned against us, and we went on quietly with our work until the public frenzy subsided."

The anti-Chinese protests, encouraged by labor leaders, had an effect. In 1882 Congress passed the Chinese Exclusion Act, which barred Chinese laborers from entering the country for the next ten years. Teachers, students, merchants, and travelers were allowed entry. In 1892 the law was extended for another ten years. Then the exclusion was made permanent.

THE GARMENT INDUSTRY

Before the Civil War, most men's clothing was made by tailors or at home. When the soldiers found that ready-made military clothing fit them well, they were willing to buy ready-made clothes for civilian use after the war. This created a demand that set the textile mills working overtime and created the new business of manufacturing ready-to-wear clothes.

A Czech wedding in Texas. When couples got married they often mixed American customs with those of the homeland.

Recruiting agents from New England mills went to Canada, looking for workers. They paid cash bonuses, and French Canadians headed south to cities such as Lowell and Lawrence, Massachusetts; Woonsocket, Rhode Island; Lewiston, Maine; and Manchester, New Hampshire.

The newest immigrants

usually got the worst assignments and worked long hours — from six in the morning to six in the evening, with time off only for lunch. The mills were hot, the noise of the machines was deafening, and cotton dust got into the workers' lungs, causing permanent damage.

Immigrant children worked in the mills, too. Philippe Lemay came to Lowell, in 1864, when he was only eight. "My first job as a textile worker was in the Lawrence mill Number Five, where I worked as a doffer [a worker who removed filled bobbins from spindles] for about three years." Putting children to work was often the only way for families to survive, because wages were so low.

POLITICS

Immigrants were finally becoming more powerful in politics. The Irish, who settled in the cities, made their numbers count. They controlled Tammany Hall, the Democratic party machine in New York City. Tammany pushed for immigrant issues, obtaining funding for Catholic schools, orphanages, and hospitals.

Most importantly, Tammany's leaders controlled the awarding of jobs in the city's government, from police officers to city commissioners. It maintained a political leader in every neighborhood, to whom people could go if they needed a job or some other kind of aid. Providing patronage of this kind kept the organization in power, for on election day the local leader saw to it that all loyal Democrats went to the polls. Indeed, the Tammany machine was waiting for new immigrants at Castle Garden, ready to sign them up as members of the Democratic party.

Tammany Hall's control of Castle Garden led to demands for reform. In 1890 the federal government completely took over the processing of immigrants. The United States decided to build a new national receiving station at Ellis Island. It would open two years later — not a moment too soon. The number of immigrants was about to skyrocket.

The Lady in the Harbor

In 1871 a French sculptor, Frédéric-Auguste Bartholdi, became interested in a plan to build a statue to commemorate the centennial of the United States. The French were to pay for the statue's construction, and the Americans would donate a site and a pedestal for the statue.

While Bartholdi and a team of skilled metalworkers labored on the statue, the fund-raising effort went slowly. Finally Joseph Pulitzer, an immigrant from Hungary who was publisher of the popular New York *World*, urged his readers to contribute their nickels and dimes for the pedestal. Bedloe's Island in New York harbor was chosen as the site. The island had been named after Isaac Bedloe, a Huguenot immigrant who grazed cows there in the 1650s.

Finally, in October 1886, President Grover Cleveland dedicated the statue. At 151 feet high, it was the tallest statue in the world. In the next few decades the largest wave of European immigrants arrived, passing by it as they sailed into New York. The "Lady in the Harbor" — today known as the Statue of Liberty — was for many their first sight of the United States. It became a symbol of the freedom and opportunity that immigrants could find here.

CHAPTER SEVEN

STREETS PAVED WITH GOLD

Stoyan Christowe was a Bulgarian born in the Balkan mountains
of southeast Europe. He described how a man named Michael Gurkin
became "the Christopher Columbus of our village." Gurkin's stories
made Christowe want to come to America.

*"He kept twirling his immense mustachios, the only thing about him which
America had not changed. All stared at him, all listened spellbound to his
giddy tales of buildings that scratched the sky, buildings, mind you, without
stairways in them, but with the rooms themselves moving up and down and
letting you off or picking you up at any floor you liked. . . .*

"'Go ahead, Michael, tell us more,' they cried.

*"Gurkin . . . related wonder after wonder, miracle after miracle, things one
never heard of, not even in the folk tales. He told how by the mere touching of
a button a whole house, yea, a whole city, was lighted, and not by kerosene
lamps or gas lights, but by 'elektritchestvo.' . . .*

"'And what might that be, Michael?'

*"Michael thought a moment, then his eyes lit up and he said confidently,
'Elektritchestvo is something which burns and gives light, more light than any
kerosene lamp could ever give. It is not a flame, and you can't blow it out no
matter how hard you try.'"*

Michael Gurkin was not exaggerating. Electricity lit up the cities of America at night; the moving rooms were elevators. Exploding economic growth was making the United States the leading industrial power in the world. Immigrants played an important part in the country's success. In the period from 1890 to 1917, tales like Michael's drew about 15 million immigrants to the United States. It was the greatest influx of new Americans until the 1990s.

Immigrant children, particularly those from southern and eastern Europe, worked in the mines.
Though some children were as young as seven, their jobs were often very dangerous and the
work hours very long.

In 1896, for the first time, the majority of European immigrants came from eastern and southern Europe, rather than from the north and west. They were primarily Slavs, Jews, Hungarians, Finns, Italians, and Greeks. Germans, Scandinavians, Irish, people from the British Isles, and other northern Europeans kept coming, too, but in smaller numbers than before.

They came to work in factories and mines, favoring cities over rural areas. Many planned to return home after making some money. The majority were male and tended to be Catholic and Jewish, rather than Protestant. These were the so-called new immigrants.

Waving good-bye to Italy. Leaving home and loved ones, probably never to see them again, was always a sad experience.

Millions came from the Russian Empire. Jews formed the largest group. By 1914 more than 2 million had arrived, many fleeing because of religious persecution. In the Russian Empire, Jews were forced to live within a restricted area called the Jewish Pale. Jews were victims of attacks called *pogroms.* Government authorities stood by or cooperated while Russian peasants burned Jewish villages and killed their inhabitants. Most Jewish immigrants came here to settle permanently. "I never planned to go to Russia again. Never!" said Celia Soloway. "I had a bad life in Europe. That's why I came here."

Poles, Ukranians, Finns, and Germans also left the Russian Empire. Opportunity and freedom attracted many. John Kuivala, a Finn, said, "I came to get a little butter on top of the bread." A traveler to Poland who visited a

Who Was Coming

The Top Nations
1891–1900: Total,
3,687,564;
Italy — 651,893;
Austro-Hungarian
Empire — 592,707;
Russian Empire — 505,290;
Germany — 505,152;
Ireland — 388, 416.
1901–1910: Total,
8,795,386;
Austro-Hungarian
Empire — 2,145,266;
Italy, 2,045,877;
Russian Empire —
1,597,306;
United Kingdom —
341,408;
Germany — 341,498.
1911–1920: Total,
5,735,811;
Italy — 1,109,524;
Russian Empire — 921,201;
Austro-Hungarian
Empire — 896,342;
Canada — 742,185;
United Kingdom —341,408;
Greece — 184,201;
Ireland — 146,181.

peasant school said that the best student, when asked where America was, answered, "It was the country to which good Polish boys went when they died." A sprinkling of ethnic Russians also emigrated, leaving their mark in the names of such towns as Moscow, Idaho; and Odessa, in both Texas and Washington. Romanians also came from Eastern Europe.

The Austro-Hungarian Empire occupied most of Central Europe. It had a population of many ethnic and national groups. Among them were Poles, Jews, Serbs, Croatians, Slovenes, Czechs, Slovaks, Austrians, and Hungarians. Many of these people resented the domination of their overlords and sought greater freedom in America. John Szabo of Hungary, who came to Chicago, expressed it well: "I always had the feeling that . . . I am not quite the human being I have the right to be. . . . Thus I emigrated and learned to know America, the land of Liberty."

This Hungarian mother and her children are probably joining the father who is already in America.

From the south of Europe came the largest single group of new immigrants — Italians. Carla Martinelli noted, "There was nothing in Italy, nothing in Italy. That's why we came. To find work, because Italy didn't have no work. Mama used to say, 'America is rich, America is rich.'"

Also arriving from southern Europe were Greeks, Spaniards, and Portuguese. With the Portuguese came people from Portugal's colony of Cape Verde — the only voluntary African immigrants till modern times. Greeks, Armenians, and Syrians who lived within the Ottoman Empire also headed for the United States. The Armenians were fleeing terrible persecution by the Turkish government, which had begun a policy of genocide toward the Armenians in 1895.

ASIAN NEWCOMERS

New immigrants came from Asia as well. After the Chinese Exclusion Act halted the immigration of Chinese workers, Japanese immigrants took their places. The first seventy-five Japanese workers were brought to California in 1888 for the harvest. Within twenty years more than 150,000 Japanese men and women arrived.

Small numbers of Indians and Koreans also arrived. Men

A Japanese family at the Honolulu entry depot. Japanese worked in Hawaii before it became part of the United States.

from the Punjab area of western India, pushed by years of famine, came to Washington, Oregon, and the farmlands of California, to find agricultural jobs.

LEAVING HOME

All immigrants left home with hopes for the future. Irja Laaksonen, who came from Finland, wrote in her diary the night she left: "Except for the sleigh bells and the muffled thud of the horses' hooves on the snowy street, the night was silent and dark as pitch. The stars in the Milky Way seemed to blink their goodbyes to us. 'Mama,' I cried, 'the stars are following us. Are they going to America too?' Mama said yes, the stars would be there too."

This Serbian grandmother cheerfully faced the future. She was one of thousands of people who came here from the Balkans in the early twentieth century.

Mary Antin, an immigrant from Russia, remembered her last night at home: "We slept at my uncle's house, having disposed of all our belongings. . . . I did not really sleep. Excitement kept me awake, and my aunt snored hideously. In the morning I was going away from Polotzk, forever and ever. I was going on a wonderful journey. I was going to America. How could I sleep?"

The journey from Europe to America was faster, cheaper, and safer than it had ever been before. By 1890 the time it took a ship to cross the Atlantic was down to as little as eight days. Prices were slashed so that an immigrant could travel in the cheapest level of steerage for a fare as low as twenty-five to thirty-five dollars.

Regular passenger service across the Pacific became established as well. The trip took eighteen or nineteen days. Chiyokichi Kyono, who departed from Kobe, Japan, had her first taste of American food on board ship. "One morning," she recalled, "square slices of bread were served with a yellow lump. I thought it must be some kind of radish pickle, and carelessly I put the yellow lump into my mouth. Ugh! I still remember that I spontaneously uttered a sound similar to a scream. It was butter, not one bit like a radish pickle! To tell the truth I had never before met up with such a material as 'butter.' It melted in my mouth, felt sticky, and I couldn't stand the smell."

Immigrants arrived at Ellis Island with only their most important possessions in their suitcases and dreams for their future.

In 1891 the federal government took over the processing of immigrants. It appointed a Superintendent of Immigration and set up twenty-four inspection stations as the only legal ports of entry. The Atlantic entry points included New York, Baltimore, Philadelphia, Providence, and Boston; on the West Coast, the entry points were Seattle and San Francisco. Other immigrant stations were at Galveston, Texas, and New Orleans.

The new immigration law set health qualifications for entry and established a Marine Hospital Service to conduct medical inspections on new arrivals. It also established an enforcement agency that would later become the Immigration and Naturalization Service.

ARRIVING AT ELLIS ISLAND

The busiest entry point was Ellis Island in New York Harbor, which opened in 1892. On arrival in New York, ships docked at the Hudson or East River piers. Holders of first- and second-class tickets were quickly examined by doctors and inspectors aboard the ship. Then they would disembark and, after passing through customs at the piers, were free to enter the United States. Only if they appeared to have legal or medical problems were they forced to go through Ellis Island as well.

However, all third-class and steerage passengers were required to go to Ellis Island for examination. They were carefully tagged with their names and the name of the vessel on which they had arrived. William Nickinovich, who came from Montenegro, now part of Yugoslavia, as a young boy with his mother, remembered her insisting, "Don't you leave me. You hold my hand all the time."

Men and women lined up separately for examinations by members of the U.S. Public Health Service. The first were "eye men" looking for cataracts, conjunctivitis, or trachoma — three diseases that

Spending the Night at Ellis Island

Louis Adamic came to the United States from Slovenia in 1913. He described his first night on Ellis Island:

"The first night in America I spent, with hundreds of other recently arrived immigrants, in an immense hall with tiers of narrow iron-and-canvas bunks, four deep. I was assigned a top bunk. Unlike some of the steerage immigrants, I had no bedding with me, and the blanket which someone threw at me was too thin to be effective against the blasts of cold air that rushed in through the open windows; so that I shivered, sleepless, all night, listening to snores and dream-monologues in perhaps a dozen different languages.

"The bunk immediately beneath mine was occupied by a Turk, who slept with his turban wound around his head. He was tall, thin, dark, bearded, hollow-faced and hook-nosed. At peace with Allah, he snored all night, producing a thin wheezing sound, which occasionally, for a moment or two, took on a deeper note.

"I thought how curious it was that I should be spending a night in such proximity to a Turk, for Turks were traditional enemies of Balkan peoples, including my own nation. For centuries Turks had forayed into Slovenian territory. Now here I was, trying to sleep directly above a Turk, with only a sheet of canvas between us."

guaranteed passage on the next ship back to Europe. The line continued on past more doctors looking for mental deficiencies, insanity, signs of pregnancy, favus (a contagious scalp disease), and physical abnormalities. Doctors looked for unusual behavior that might indicate mental illness — including excessive smiling or nail biting. If a doctor saw any signs of these, he would make a chalk mark on the immigrant's clothing: *pg* for pregnant; *k* for hernia; *h* for heart; *x* for mental illness. Immigrants with the dreaded chalk marks were taken away for further examination.

Those who passed the medical exam went up to the second floor to the Great Hall. Here the immigrant had to answer an inspector's questions about forms they had filled out before boarding the ships. Louis Adamic, a Slovene, remembered: "The official spoke a bewildering variety of many Slavic languages. He had a stern voice and a sour visage. I had difficulty understanding some of his questions." If the immigrant could not answer the questions, he or she was put in detention for further grilling.

Many immigrants wore their native costume, like this Albanian woman from Italy who arrived at Ellis Island in 1905.

This young Finnish man arrived at Ellis Island as a stowaway. Immigrants took many risks to reach the United States.

In the dreaded eye exam, the Ellis Island inspector rolled back the immigrant's eyelids with a hook.

DETENTION AND REJECTION

Detention at Ellis Island could last hours or days or longer. Those who arrived without money were not permitted to leave the island until someone brought them money or vouched for them with a bond. Women and children traveling alone were always detained until a male relative came for them. Maljan Chavoor, a young boy from Turkey, recalled being in detention with his mother: "The first night they gave me two blankets and said, 'You go with the men.' My mother went with the women. They put us in a cell. Boom! I was only eleven. . . . I cried all night. . . . Twenty-one days our case was being heard and tried."

Lillian Davis Katz had a happier experience when she arrived with her mother and brother. "The first night they were celebrating Christmas. They had a movie. I had never seen one. And there was Santa Claus. And we got tiny little gifts. All the beauty of Christmas suddenly hit me. . . . I ate my first hot dog and my first banana there. These were revelations. Very exciting for this little kid."

Only about 2 percent of the new arrivals were turned back. The greatest tragedy came about when one member of the family was refused entry. Then the family had to choose between letting that one return home alone, or having everyone go back to the homeland.

FINDING A PLACE TO LIVE

For those who planned to stay in New York, the ordeal was over after passing through Ellis Island. Friends or relatives often met the new immigrants.

A man from Syria remembered, "My uncle had a friend who met us at Ellis Island and helped to get us quickly out of the vessel, and ten hours later after we had come into the bay we were established in two rooms in the third story of a brick house in Washington Street, only three blocks from Battery Park."

Others took the train to points west. Tags that were pinned to immigrants' clothing on the boat included their final destination. Evelyn Berkowitz came from Hungary to Braddock, Pennsylvania, with her family when she was twelve. "We looked very immigrant," she remembered. "And we turned a corner and some children were coming home from school for lunch hour, and they started yelling, 'Greenhorns! Greenhorns!' and throwing snowballs at us. My dad got so angry. But then my mother's sister saw us through the window, and came running down."

The roof on Ellis Island had a play area for children of detained people. These kids ride an Uncle Sam wagon around 1910.

CHINESE AT ANGEL ISLAND

From 1910 to 1940, the primary immigrant receiving station on the West Coast was Angel Island in San Francisco Harbor. The officials at Angel Island were as devoted to keeping people out as they were to welcoming immigrants to the new country.

The Chinese Exclusion Act made some Chinese illegal immigrants. The Act did not cut off all Chinese immigration; it only excluded laborers. The challenge for the potential Chinese immigrant was to show that he was really a merchant, rather than a laborer.

Arrivals who could not prove this were detained, sometimes for weeks or months or even longer.

Another way for Chinese immigrants to get into the country was to prove they were sons of a Chinese citizen. Although Chinese could not be naturalized as citizens, those born in the United States were automatically citizens, just like anyone else born here. Any child of theirs was eligible to enter the United States. So sometimes young men in China would buy papers that would show they were sons of a United States–Chinese citizen. These people were called "paper sons."

Their number increased after the great San Francisco earthquake of 1906. In the quake's aftermath, a large fire destroyed the building where the birth records were stored. It now became impossible to know who exactly had been born in the United States and who in China.

At Angel Island inspectors asked very detailed questions about immigrants' houses and neighbors in China, trying to trip them up. Many Chinese "paper sons" prepared for the voyage across the Pacific by memorizing briefing books about their false family backgrounds and community.

PICTURE BRIDES

After 1907 Japanese women began to arrive in larger numbers. In that year an informal agreement between the governments of Japan and the United States (the "Gentlemen's Agreement") restricted the entrance of any more Japanese laborers. The Agreement permitted Japanese men already in the United States to bring Japanese wives from home. Usually these wives were "picture brides." Their marriages were arranged by exchanging photographs. The man sent his picture to a family member or professional marriage broker, who then sent back a photo of a woman

A Japanese couple exchanged these pictures. This picture bride came to America with just the young man's picture to start a new life.

A Japanese Bride Arrives in America

Hanayo Inouye grew up in a middle-class home in Japan. She married a Japanese man visiting her village from America. She described her first experiences when he took her back:

"When I arrived . . . my husband said, 'We are going to the country. You'd better not put good clothes on.' When we got to the farm, Mr. Omaye showed me around and said, 'Please make yourself comfortable in here.' I couldn't be more surprised! He motioned to a corner of the barn where there was hay spread in a square shape with a partition! That was all there was! I certainly did not feel like taking off my clothes and napping there. I never felt more distressed in my whole life. My husband should have told me about such conditions before I left Japan. He had shown me some pictures of himself in suits and of nothing but the best scenery. Naturally, I thought I was coming to a really nice place when I left Japan. I might have taken it differently had I been raised in a less fortunate family.

"When I asked my husband where the toilet was, he pointed outside. It was out in the field. He told me to hit the toilet with a stick before going in . . . [as] there were black spiders living in it. . . . Many people were bitten by those black spiders, and I heard someone died of a fever caused by the spider bites. I was quite scared of the place. I realized, however, that no matter how much I thought of my mother back in Japan or of anybody, it wouldn't do any good. I knew then I had to live with it and give it a try. But I told myself I was going back home as soon as I made some money here."

who wanted a husband. Arranged marriages were not unique to the Japanese; many other immigrant groups used friends or relatives to find brides from their home country.

Japanese picture brides arrived here naturally curious about what their husbands would be like. Some men had sent photos of themselves when they were much younger. Others represented themselves as wealthier than they were. Hideyo Yokoyama, who arrived in Seattle as a picture bride, remembered: "My husband was 13 years older than I. I had heard that he was a dentist, but I found out he was a truck driver. . . . I wanted to go back to Japan as soon as possible. But I had no money for a ticket to return. So I was caught by fate and consigned to live in America permanently."

Inspectors on Angel Island really grilled Chinese immigrants to see if they would be allowed to enter the country.

GOING TO WORK

New immigrants who had no specific job skills worked on the same type of construction projects that the Irish had earlier. "I came to America," an Italian immigrant was said to have remarked, "because I heard the streets were paved with gold. When I got here, I found out three things: First, the streets weren't paved with gold; second, they weren't paved at all; and third, I was expected to pave them." There were many such jobs available. Immigrants built the skyscrapers, roads, bridges, tunnels, subways, and sewers of the nation's great cities.

Often Italian work crews were assembled and run by a fellow-Italian, called a *padrone*. Because he knew some English, the padrone could deal with the bosses. He recruited the workers and was responsible for getting them to the work site. He also paid them — often taking a very large cut for himself. Greek and Syrian work crews also used the padrone system.

THE GARMENT TRADE

The clothing business grew with the help of immigrant labor. Jewish and Italian workers toiled for long hours and low pay in urban tenement workplaces called sweatshops. Marie Ganz recalled: "We sat in long rows, our bodies bent over the machines, the work we turned out fell into wooden bins attached to the part of the machine facing us. No one girl made an entire garment. As each girl completed her part the garment was passed on to the next girl. . . . At the end of the week the girl who had turned in the least work was dropped from the payroll."

Throughout New England, the textile mills continued to use immigrant labor. Italian, Polish, Russian, Greek, Syrian, and Portuguese workers followed in the footsteps of the Irish and French Canadians. The hours were long, with ten- to twelve-hour days, six days a week. The mills were poorly ventilated, and the clouds of fiber dust made the work unhealthy. Work often started at seven, which meant that women

Mina Kawamoto sewed clothes at home in California around 1900. The garment trade was then booming.

Working for a Padrone

Rocco Corresca, a young Italian immigrant, was recruited for work by a padrone at Ellis Island. He described his experience:

"We came to Brooklyn, New York, to a wooden house in Adams Street that was full of Italians from Naples. Bartolo [the padrone] had a room on the third floor and there were fifteen men in the room, all boarding with Bartolo. . . .

"The next morning, early, Bartolo told us to go out and pick rags and get bottles. He gave us bags and hooks and showed us the ash barrels. On the streets where the fine houses are, the people are very careless and put out good things, like mattresses and umbrellas, clothes, hats, and boots. We brought all these to Bartolo, and he made them new again and sold them on the sidewalk. But mostly we brought back rags and bones. The rags we had to wash in the back yard and then we hung them to dry on lines under the ceiling in our room. The bones we kept under the beds till Bartolo could find a man to buy them.

"Most of the men in our room worked at digging the sewer. Bartolo got them the work and they paid him about one quarter of their wages. Then he charged them for board and he bought the clothes for them, too. So they got little money after all. Bartolo was always saying that the rent of the room was so high that he could not make anything, but he was really making plenty. He was what they call a padrone and is now a very rich man. The men that were living with him had just come to America and could not speak English — Bartolo told us all that we must work for him and that if we did not the police would come and put us in prison. . . .

"We were with Bartolo nearly a year, but some of our countrymen who had been in the place a long time said that Bartolo had no right to us and we could get work for a dollar and a half a day, which, when you make it lire [Italian currency], is very much. So we went away one day to Newark and got work on the street. Bartolo came after us and made a great noise, but the boss said that if he did not go away soon the police would have him. Then he went, saying that there was no justice in the country."

had to rise at four-thirty to prepare breakfast and do their household chores. One Portuguese immigrant remarked, "My life in America has been constantly to work."

MINES AND STOCKYARDS

Early immigrant miners needed skills and experience. By the late nineteenth century, however, new technology had mechanized the work and most mining jobs were unskilled. But the pay was still high enough to attract new immigrants from Eastern Europe — particularly Poles, Slovaks, Hungarians, Slovenes, and Serbs.

Working in a Sweatshop

Sadie Frowne, who came from Poland, described her job in a sweatshop:

"At seven o'clock we all sit down to our machines and the boss brings to each one the pile of work that he or she is to finish during the day, what they call in English their 'stint.' This pile is put down beside the machine, and as soon as a skirt is done it is laid on the other side of the machine. Sometimes the work is not all finished by six o'clock, and then the one who is behind must work overtime. Sometimes one is finished ahead of time and gets away at four or five o'clock, but generally we are not done till six o'clock.

"The machines go like mad all day, because the faster you work the more money you get.

Sometimes in my haste I get my finger caught and the needle goes right through it. It goes so quick, though, that it does not hurt much. I bind the finger up with a piece of cotton and go on working. We all have accidents like that. Where the needle goes through the nail it makes a sore finger, or where it splinters a bone it does much harm. Sometimes a finger has to come off. Generally, though, one can be cured by salve.

"All the time we are working, the boss walks about examining the finished garments and making us do them over again if they are not just right. So we have to be careful as well as swift."

Coal and iron ore from the mines were shipped through the Great Lakes to steel mills in the Midwest. This combination made the United States the world's leading producer of steel in the early twentieth century. Immigrants formed the labor force of the steel mills as well as the mines.

Martin Dekrovich, who went to Pittsburgh, remembered: "You could make more money there working in a foundry. But it was not very attractive. Three or four big, strong fellows from my town used to work in those foundries, taking sand off the casting. They were making [good money]. But all four died between thirty and forty years of age because they got too much sand in their lungs. . . . So I said to myself, 'Well this is not the job for me. I didn't come to America to kill myself. I came to America to make money.' So I quit that job and went to New York."

The stockyards of Chicago attracted Poles, Lithuanians, and other Slavic groups. The work was grim, as a Lithuanian described: "My job was in the cattle killing room. I pushed the blood along the gutter. . . . The cattle do not suffer. They are knocked senseless with a big hammer and are dead before they wake up. . . . One Lithuanian who worked with me, said, 'They get all the blood out of those cattle and all the work out of us men.'"

WOMEN'S AND CHILDREN'S WORK

Most immigrant jobs did not pay enough to support a family. As a result, women and children also had to work. Edward Corsi, an Italian immigrant, remembered: "When I was old enough for my first job, I went to work as a lamplighter, rising at four in the morning to put out the lamps on my route. Then I would have breakfast and get to school by nine o'clock. All through my boyhood I worked at various odd jobs, paying my way through school and at the same time contributing what little I could to the limited family income. I was, in turn, lamplighter, messenger, and clerk in a telegraph office."

Immigrant girls usually worked as domestic helpers, or took care of younger children at home to free their mothers to work elsewhere. Immigrant boys were more likely to work outside. They took street jobs collecting items for the junk man. Sometimes they scavenged the rail lines and alleys and construction sites and around docks, picking up scraps and coal that had fallen. Often they stole coal and wood for home fuel. Many shined shoes for a living. Peddling newspapers was the classic children's job, and both boys and girls took part.

Children worked at dangerous jobs. In the glass factories of Pennsylvania, young boys were "carrier pigeons," who had to carry three or four red-hot bottles on an asbestos shovel to the annealing oven. Young workers in many

Selling newspapers was a popular job for kids. These Greek immigrant boys were selling a Greek-language newspaper.

Many immigrants worked in the meatpacking business centered in the Chicago area. These Polish workers are making sausage.

Jewish immigrants played an important role in organizing unions. These teenagers protested conditions in the garment industry.

factories breathed poisonous fumes. Immigrant children working in mines suffered accidents at three times the rate of adults. Some states prohibited children under sixteen from underground work. But children who were younger worked above ground, hunched over conveyor belts, separating coal from unwanted slate. The belts moved along quickly, raising dust that caused lung disease.

Women in immigrant communities often ran boardinghouses. This was backbreaking work. It required cleaning, washing clothes, making beds, and fixing meals. Besides a large breakfast for the boarders, the owner had to send each man off with a full lunch pail and have dinner ready when he returned. The pay, though, could be very good. In the western mining towns, it was possible for a woman to make more than a man, if she had enough boarders.

Bohemian and Slovak women were famous for their expert lacework and embroidery. Italian women and children also made lace and other decorations that were sewn on clothing made in sweatshops. Children could work before and after school; their small hands made them useful for clipping, sorting, painting, pasting, stringing, or sewing tiny items. Their pay was almost equally small. In Providence, Rhode Island, where many Italians lived, one study showed that almost half of all children were working before the age of eleven.

AGRICULTURAL WORK

Immigrant labor has always kept the prices of food low. Farmers depended on immigrants to plant and harvest the crops. In Colorado, the sugar-beet industry employed Germans from Russia and Mexicans. Beet growing had two bursts of activity. In the spring the crop had to be thinned, and in the fall the crop was pulled and topped. During the seasonal peaks, children from the age of eight worked nine to thirteen hours a day with their families. The children worked unpaid for their parents.

Japanese farmworkers developed truck farming in California by growing strawberries and other fruits and vegetables. In time, many Japanese Americans managed to save money to buy land. But their success made them targets of prejudice. In 1913 the state passed the Alien Land Law, which prohibited people "ineligible for citizenship" (Asians) from owning land.

Indian and Mexican immigrants worked the agricultural circuit in California as well. First they harvested the orchards, vineyards, and sugar-beet fields of northern California. From there they worked in the citrus groves of central California, and finally, following the annual sequence of harvests, in the cantaloupe fields and cotton fields of the southern Imperial Valley.

New England had its agricultural season as well. Poles and other Eastern Europeans were usually hired on for a season of eight months — the time of outdoor work on the farm. They were paid eighty dollars a month, from which they had to pay the agent who got them the job. But since they received room and board on the farm, many were able to save enough to purchase their own land.

Armenians working in California fields picking grapes. They pioneered the raisin industry in Fresno.

Cape Verdean immigrants introduced the strawberry to Cape Cod. Elmira Nunes Lopes remembered: "We would pick strawberries from about four o'clock in the morning until . . . the sun is high and hot, the strawberries tend to crust so easily." As the summer waned the fruit pickers harvested blueberries in the woods. In September, they returned to the cranberry bogs for the harvest.

CHAPTER EIGHT

IMMIGRANT COMMUNITIES

Rose Gollup, a Russian Jew, came to the United States in 1891 from a village in today's Belarus. Rose described her mother's adjustment to the new country:

"Mother had been here only a short time when I noticed that she looked older and more old-fashioned than father. I noticed that it was so with most of our women, especially those that wore wigs or kerchiefs on their heads. So I thought that if I could persuade her to leave off her kerchief she would look younger and more up-to-date. . . . So, one day . . . I asked her playfully to take off her kerchief and let me do her hair, just to see how it would look. She consented reluctantly. She had never before in her married life had her hair uncovered before anyone. I took off her kerchief and began to fuss with her hair. It was dark and not abundant but it was soft and had a pretty wave in it. When I parted it in front and gathered it in a small knot in the middle of the back of her head, leaving it soft over the temples, I was surprised how different she looked. . . .

"When father came home in the evening and caught sight of her while still at the door, he stopped and looked at her with astonishment. 'What!' he cried, half earnestly, half jestingly. 'Already you are becoming an American lady!' Mother looked abashed for a moment; in the next, to my surprise and delight, I heard her brazen it out in her quiet way.

"'As you see,' she said, 'I am not staying far behind.'"

Rose's mother adapted to American customs quite rapidly. But people often had a hard time. Immigrants found the adjustment easier if they lived near others from the same homeland. In these neighborhoods, they could hear their native language, shop at stores where familiar foods and other items were available, and not feel out of place.

Waving American flags and cheering, Germans from Russia greet President Theodore Roosevelt on a visit to Kansas. The chance to see the leader of their new country was a special thrill for immigrants.

ℕEIGHBORHOODS

Immigrant kids playing in the street in New York City. It often took days before dead horses were removed.

Most of the new immigrants settled in cities. The neighborhoods where they lived sometimes got nicknames that showed where the people came from. Little Italies, Greektowns, Polonias, Chinatowns, and Little Bohemias dotted cities from Massachusetts to California.

These neighborhoods served as a haven from the strange and hostile world beyond. Here, no immigrant ever felt "different." Abraham Rihbany described the Syrian colony in New York as "providing me with a home . . . among those whose language was my language and whose habits were my habits."

There were many social clubs in these neighborhoods. A newcomer could often find one whose members were all from the same village or district that he or she had come from. At meetings, they could exchange news from the homeland and learn about available jobs. Some clubs collected dues that were used to provide help to members who were out of work or to pay benefits to the families of members who died.

NEW YORK CITY

The largest number of new immigrants settled in New York. Jews from Eastern Europe, who formed the biggest group, settled on the Lower East Side of Manhattan. By 1910 almost one fourth of the population of New York City lived in this area — perhaps the most densely populated one-and-a-half square miles on Earth. Peddlers with pushcarts and merchants at outdoor stalls sold almost every kind of item. Shops with Yiddish signs dotted the streets, and the aroma of kosher foods from Eastern Europe filled the air. The neighborhood included steam baths, Yiddish theaters, and crowded tenement buildings.

"We all lived in tenements," remembered Abe Beame, who came to the Lower East Side as an infant in 1906. (He grew up to become the first Jewish mayor of New York City.) "You had a living room, a kitchen, and one or two bedrooms. I remember we used to sleep three to a bed. I slept with my two brothers. The tenements were heated by coal. But you had to buy your own coal and your own ice to put in the icebox. . . . The apartments were lit by gaslight. The toilet was down the hall. You shared it with the other apartments. I remember one place I lived where the toilet was an outhouse in the yard."

Some immigrant neighborhoods included people from several different cultures. James Karavolas came to New York from Greece. His family of six settled in a section of the city called Hell's Kitchen. "It was a tough neighborhood," he recalled. "Some blocks were just the Greek neighborhood. Another block was the Italian neighborhood, Spanish neighborhood. I used to help the lamplighter on Twenty-second Street. . . . And there was a market: vegetables, fruits, meat, poultry. Milk was delivered by horse and wagon on cobblestone streets."

Everyone in this social gathering of 1916 came from the village of Mushghura in Lebanon. Chain migration was at work here.

Many Eastern European immigrants lived in rooming houses. These workers in the Pittsburgh area relax with music.

CHICAGO AND PITTSBURGH

The population of Chicago also swelled with newcomers around the turn of the century. There was already a Polish community in the northwest part of the city, and many thousands of new Polish immigrants headed there after arriving in the United States. Because many of the Poles who immigrated were of peasant background and had migrated from the farm to the factory, they tried to make their communities in the United States as much like an Old World village as possible. The Chicago Polonia (people of Polish descent living outside Poland) was the largest in the country. In 1900 more Poles lived in Chicago than in any other city except Warsaw, the capital of Poland itself.

Pittsburgh was home to many Eastern Europeans who worked in the mines and steel factories. The houses were jammed together and often empty of furniture, with just a bundle of shawls and a pile of straw for bedding. Because these new immigrants planned to return to their home countries after earning money, they had little interest in house furnishings. Many were single men who lived in boardinghouses. The woman in charge, sometimes the wife of an immigrant herself, was responsible for cooking such favorites as cabbage soup and for washing the men's clothes. In return, she and her children, if any, lived free of rent. She often had to wash the backs of the men in their hot baths — definitely necessary after a long, dirty day in the mills and mines.

CHINATOWNS AND LITTLE TOKYOS

Chinatowns grew up in San Francisco, New York, and Boston. A Chinese immigrant expressed the importance of Chinatown: "It is only in Chinatown that a Chinese immigrant has society, friends, and relatives who share his dreams and hopes, his hardships and adventures. Here he can tell a joke and make everybody laugh with him; here he may hear folktales told which create the illusion that Chinatown is really China." Chinatowns usually had few women and children because Chinese immigration had been virtually halted and discrimination

"Dog Killers"

Mrs. Riyo Orite came to Wyoming from Japan to join her husband who was a section head on a railroad. She was expected to do the cooking for the railroad laborers — ten people altogether, including Mexicans and Italians as well as Japanese. She knew nothing about western cooking when she arrived.

"Now I talk about the past and laugh, but then . . . I remember the time I learned to bake biscuits for the workers' lunches because of the rice shortage. I was taught how to make them by one of the workers. I kneaded the batter and shaped it into balls. The oven at that time didn't have a temperature indicator, so I just put in my hand. If it felt hot, it was good enough. I opened the oven after ten minutes and found that the dumplings weren't done yet. I checked on them a few times before they were done. Then they got harder. I cracked one of them again and found it was well done. All right, so I wrapped them in a cloth, but I didn't serve them for dinner. I put them in a box for lunch on the following day. I also put in a can of sardines for each person, boiled eggs, and put butter and jam on the biscuits. The men took their lunches with them. When they came back in the evening, they teased me by saying, 'Today's dog killers were delicious.' I couldn't figure out what they meant by dog killers. I asked the oldest worker, 'Did you get anything today? What's a dog killer?' He answered, 'The biscuits you baked were hard enough to hit and kill dogs with. Therefore, we named the biscuits dog killers.'

"My husband said that he couldn't crack the biscuits unless he threw them at a telephone pole. Since I was the only woman, I was teased by everybody."

had made it difficult for females to come to the United States.

Japanese settled in neighborhoods called Japantowns or Little Tokyos in Seattle, Oakland, and Los Angeles. Izo Kojimo remembered how familiar the Japanese neighborhood in Seattle seemed to him when he first arrived. It had "cafes, restaurants, Chinese restaurants, noodle shops, sushi shops, a condiments store, a tofu store, groceries, drugstores, a pool hall, ten-cent stores . . . One couldn't believe he was abroad, and one didn't even need to speak English."

Proudly marching with banners, Lithuanians celebrate their heritage in their new home in Lawrence, Massachusetts.

These Japanese families were playing tug-of-war at a picnic in the Fresno area of California around 1910.

Immigration put strains on families. Many immigrants were men who arrived alone. They worked to bring their wives and children over later. After years of separation many couples seemed like strangers to each other. Once women experienced the freedoms of the United States, they were less likely to want to be submissive to their husbands in the Old World way. An advice book for Italian immigrants of 1911 warned men, "It is a crime severely punished in all states for a man to strike his wife. . . . Treat women and children very kindly." Usually the grandparents were left behind, so the family was incomplete.

FINDING A MATE

Unmarried young men and women usually wanted to marry within their own group. "He must be Hungarian," was the advice given to a Hungarian immigrant woman by her family. Maria Tovas remembered: "There was a big Greek population in Lowell [Massachusetts]. In fact my husband was from the same village as me and he was in Lowell. I recognized him because he used to come to my father's saddle store. One time my father saw him and he said to his father, 'You have a good-looking son.' Then he said, 'Listen, I have three daughters. Some day I want to make you my son-in-law.'"

Almost all immigrant groups had social events where young people could meet. Edna Vidravich Balkus met her husband at one. "I met him in a dance," she remembered. "We go . . . every Saturday . . . [It was] full of people, all Lithuanian, nobody else. . . . They make a party, all people go, spend the evening, you know, it's nice."

Young unmarried men who came to the United States often returned home for a bride or sent for one from the Old Country.

Sometimes the bride and groom had known each other before; other times they were known only through friends or family members. Some women in the Old Country regarded American emigrants as a real catch. A Polish observer noted, "They [the brides] risk going alone to America while they are often afraid to go alone to the nearest town in their own country."

Many of the new immigrants came from cultures where the family of the bride had to provide a dowry, or payment, to the groom. In Croatia, custom demanded that the girl provide clothing for herself and her husband as well as stockings for life. In the Greek culture, many times the brothers in the family had to work to earn money for their sister's dowry. Labor investigators found that many women were working to earn their dowry. So widespread was the custom that some labor unions at the turn of the century

John Sajbel and Anna Raj chose a traditional Slovak wedding to start their new life in the Colorado Rockies.

offered dowries as part of their benefits to encourage women to join the unions. Over time the dowry custom died out.

The DeLeos, a Seattle Italian family, pose proudly with their six children. John was an early truck farmer in the area.

OLD WAYS VERSUS NEW

Immigrant children often became adjusted to the new land quickly. Sometimes they had to explain American ways to their parents. This was a reversal of the traditional role of the parent and could cause tension.

The conflict between the old ideals of the homeland and the new ideals of America were played out in the home. "Homes ceased to be places of peace," wrote Morris Raphael Cohen, who immigrated to the Lower East Side in 1892. "There was scarcely a Jewish home on the East Side that was free from this friction between parents and children."

In many immigrant families, boys were treated far less strictly than girls. Boys, for example, were often able to keep some of their earnings while daughters were required to turn all their money over to the parents. And boys were not as strictly supervised. A Hungarian girl protested, "It burns me up to think that my kid brother does all these things and has more freedom than I have, just because he is a boy. . . . My father thinks girls should not be out as much as boys, that girls should stay home, learn to cook, sew and clean the house."

Many immigrant girls were not allowed to go outside the home without adult supervision. Girls often could not see members of the opposite sex who were not family or relatives without strict supervision. An Italian women remembered her own courtship: "During the ten months we dated we were never left alone except in the parlor when I played the piano."

DIFFERENT FAMILY PATTERNS

Some immigrant groups had their own family patterns. The cultures of

Spain, Portugal, and Mexico, for example, included other people besides the parents in the raising of children. They were *compadres* and *comadres* — godparents who sponsored the newborn child at his or her baptism. A family might establish a link with another family by asking a member to become a compadre or comadre. In any case, their advice and support for the child was taken very seriously by both parents and "co-parents."

Bohemians sometimes switched traditional parental roles because the women often had the best-paying jobs in the family, working in tobacco factories. Their husbands and sons, as a result, often did some of the housework. "The boys run home from their play after school hours, to start the kitchen fire," wrote a woman social worker. "Several times I have come in to a home and found the strong young husband washing, and not at all embarassed to be caught at the washtub."

Prejudice or repressive laws created problems for certain immigrants. Many Chinese Americans had wives and children back home but few immigrants made enough money to return. The exclusion laws kept most Chinese women and children out of the United States. As a result, American Chinatowns resembled a "bachelor society."

Indian immigrants in California were also affected by laws that prohibited intermarriage between whites and nonwhites. (Asian Indians were classified as nonwhites by the law.) Since few Indian women immigrated, the men married Mexican-American women. The Mexican-Indian community developed customs that were a combination of both cultures. The children often had such names as Maria Jerusita Singh or José Akbar Khan. They combined religious traditions for marriages and celebrated the holidays of both homelands.

A Korean family in Hawaii proudly posed for a portrait. Many Koreans came to work in the sugarcane fields of the islands.

Expense was clearly no object for this Polish wedding. Pictures of such lavish events were sent to relatives in the home country.

Portuguese Americans march in the Holy Ghost parade in Lawrence, Massachusetts, in 1920. Many new immigrants of that time were Roman Catholic.

These immigrant children in Philadelphia are following the Romanian custom of putting on a skit at Christmas.

The largest religious group among the new immigrants was Roman Catholics. Their local church became an important center of immigrant life. As a Polish saying went, "Wherever there is a priest, a church, wherever a parish is being created — there Polish life grows vigorously." The churches tried to make their services as close to those in the homeland as possible. At that time, the Mass was always said in Latin. But in Polish neighborhoods the sermons would be in Polish; in Slovak ones, in Slovakian, and so on.

Each Roman Catholic immigrant group had its own patron saints from its homeland. They were the objects of special devotion. Every town in Italy had its special saint. The same was true in Portugal. The saint's feast day was an occasion for great celebration. A Portuguese immigrant to Fall River, Massachusetts, remembered: "We used to have the procession of the Feast of Saint Anthony on Saturday night. All candles. It was a beautiful sight with the original statue of Saint Anthony. It would take twenty men to carry it."

ORTHODOX JEWS

Most of the new Jewish immigrants were Orthodox Jews, who followed a strict form of their religion. In Eastern Europe, these religious practices were deeply woven into everyday life. At sundown on Friday (the beginning of the Jewish Sabbath), the shops closed. Men went to evening services at the synagogue while the women prepared — by sundown — the Sabbath dinners. The mother of the family recited the prayers and lit the Sabbath candles that light the home. At the evening meal, the father gave a prayer of thanks for the day of rest. The Jewish calendar was filled with special religious holidays starting with Rosh Hashanah.

In America, among people of many faiths and backgrounds, some Jews became less strict. When Rose Cohen joined her father in America, she was horrified to see that he used money on the Sabbath, a practice prohibited for Orthodox Jews. She wrote that when she first arrived her father bought her a melon on the Sabbath. "I saw father take his hand out of his pocket and hold out a coin. I stood staring at him for a moment. Then I dropped the melon on the pavement and ran. . . . My father had touched coin on the Sabbath! Oh, the sin!"

ASIANS

Asian immigrants in California brought their religions with them as well. The Japanese, like some Chinese, practiced Buddhism. The first Japanese in Hawaii founded a Buddhist temple there. A few years later, in 1899, they built a Buddhist temple in San Francisco. The Buddhist priests were essential to the well-being of the community. They were in charge of the ceremonies that helped people through birth, marriage, and death. They also presided over such traditional Japanese Shinto festivals as O-bon, which honored the spirits of the dead that came back to Earth for one night. Priests also wrote letters for illiterate Japanese and served as community leaders. Some Japanese became Christians after immigrating, for that was one way to become Americanized.

The Rudick family of Pittsburgh celebrate the Passover Seder in 1908.

The public schools had an enormous task in educating children from different backgrounds and cultures. All classes were in English; there were no English as a second language (ESL) programs. Most students did learn the language quite quickly. Marie Jastrow from Yugoslavia, who entered a New York school at age nine in 1908, remembered that she sat "alone and miserable. . . . I had no choice but to learn the new language, quickly and without fuss. Not much help was offered. Few teachers were linguists, and the feelings of the greenhorns in the class were not spared. This method led to miracles of accomplishment."

SCHOOL BEHAVIOR

Teachers often emphasized memorization and drill, along with recitations, organized exercises, and competitions. They had little time to

In 1910 one-third of the people of Gary, Indiana, had been born overseas. Children hold signs to show their ethnic background.

The Parochial School Day

A Polish immigrant remembered:

"In those days, the schedule of studies in a Polish parochial school was as follows: each and every day morning mass, more prayers in the classroom, followed by a few minutes of calisthenics. On alternate days this was followed by catechism and Bible history, both in Polish. Then came arithmetic in English. After recess, we had Polish reading, writing, grammar and history. The afternoons were devoted to English studies — reading, spelling, grammar, American history, and in the highest grades, literature and civics. Once a week the girls had lessons in needlework. The boys attended gym classes. I still have the pillow I made in eighth grade."

actually explain the material. In many city schools, the students recited their lessons together out loud. In Baltimore children chanted arithmetic tables and even state capitals in unison. One New York City school principal used the motto "Save the minutes." She had the students scream answers as fast as possible, the next student rising to perform while the previous one recited.

The children were forced to sit at desks, which were bolted to the floor, for the entire school day. Talking was forbidden, unless a teacher called on a student to recite. When they were not reciting, they were doing busywork. Many schools had monthly report cards, which put great strain on the children to perform. A Chicago boy complained, "When you works a whole month in school, the teacher she give you a card to take home that says how you ain't any good. And yer folks hollers on yer an' hits yer."

To make sure immigrants understood the importance of hygiene and cleanliness, health programs were part of school as well. There were regular examinations of the students' teeth and eyes and inspections for cleanliness and health. Lice probes were a common humiliation and many students long remembered their hair being explored "with two pencils" used like knitting needles. Teachers often sent home critical notes about the pupils. An Italian mother in Cleveland, on being told that her daughter needed more baths, wrote back to the teacher, "Maria is not a rose. Do not smell her, teach her!"

Both adults and youngsters attended citizenship classes in Portland, Maine. They learned English and American history.

Americanization started at the moment the immigrants landed. Usually they dressed in their finest clothes to come ashore. But they soon saw that foreign clothing marked them as "green-horns." Women in particular swiftly exchanged their clothes for American wear. Around the turn of the twentieth century, the most popular outfit for women was the shirtwaist — a blouse tailored like a man's shirt. The outfit included a long skirt with a very narrow waist. To get the look, women had to wear a tight corset. It was uncomfortable, but the sacrifice for fashion and style was acceptable.

Slavic women threw away their kerchiefs or shawls for the very popular hats of the time. In Eastern Europe, only women of high status wore hats, so this was not just a fashion statement but a woman's declaration that she was no longer a peasant. "Tell me," said a Slovak woman about her former servant, who was now an immigrant in America, "it can't be true, can it? She writes that she wears a hat. Of course even in America that is impossible."

AMERICANIZERS

Some Americans didn't think it was enough for the newcomers to adopt fresh clothing. They believed it was necessary to make the immigrants aware of American traditions and history. The goal of these "Americanizers" was assimilation, the blending of immigrants into American culture and values. Schools staged American pageants as part of the Americanization program. Sonia Walinsky, a Russian immigrant, remembered: "My brother and I were entered in school in Chicago right away. And my brother, who was ten, was surprised to see me on the stage of the auditorium of the school the first Friday we were there. There was a program, and different children were supposed to do different things, and I was supposed to wave the American flag.

I was very proud. I waved it and waved it and waved it with all my might. I thought I was really an Americanka then."

Institutions within the immigrant communities also stressed Americanization. Newspapers, for example, explained American practices in the immigrants' own languages. Peter Yolles, who came from Poland when he was nineteen, became the editor of a Polish newspaper. "On our national holidays," he wrote, "I think that we print more pictures of Washington and Lincoln, more stories of historic people and events than you will find in any American paper! New citizens are acutely interested in the problems and theories which these holidays celebrate. They have left relatives and friends behind them in troubled countries and so they are eager to read about American traditions of liberty and justice and opportunity, and we print these things, not so much as history, but as news! We treat the Constitution, and freedom of speech and equal justice for all as news, instead of as something won once and for all, a century and a half ago."

These Ukrainians in Minneapolis proved that immigrants could show pride in both their old and new homelands.

CHAPTER NINE

THE GOLDEN DOOR CLOSES

Lilly Dache, the leading woman's hat designer of her time,
came from France in 1924. At first she was disappointed.
Then she was moved by a New York experience.

*"Aimlessly I started across the street. . . . A yellow taxicab screamed to a stop not
an inch behind me. The driver leaned out of the window and shook his fist at me.*

"'Jaywalker!' he shouted. 'Wake up!'

*"I woke up, in the middle of a wild jump for the curb. . . . There was a
wonderful roar all around. It filled the air and pounded in my ears. I looked up
and saw a train thundering above me on elevated tracks. I looked down and felt
the ground beneath my feet tremble and heard the muffled roar of subway trains
below. I looked to my right and saw cars speeding north. I looked to my left and
saw cars speeding south. In the middle of the street, trolley cars clanged. . . . I
stood still, just where I was, in a narrow island in the middle of the wide street.
I looked up at the towering buildings, all around me. Here, then, were the
skyscrapers! At last! Great stores. Tall office buildings. And like a giant pulse, the
roar of traffic above me, below me, to my right and my left. I drew a deep,
intoxicating breath. All at once I was fully awake, glad to be alive. I stood in
wonder, savoring to the full the sights, the smells, the sounds. . . .*

*"The street sign above my head said, 'Herald Square.' So I stood at the
corner at 34th and Broadway, in the city of New York, and discovered America."*

Lilly Dache's delight in reaching New York was not unusual. The city already
had the most famous skyline in the world. However, prejudice against the
new immigrants had increased in the early years of the twentieth century and
would lead to a cutback in immigration. As the storm of war hit Europe, many
of these prejudices intensified.

Basilio Yomzalis from the Philippines poses with his family in Kansas.

Top Countries for Immigration

1911–1920
5,735,811
Italy — 1,109,524
Russia — 921,201
Austria-Hungary — 896,342
Canada — 742,185

1921–1930
4,107,209
Canada — 924,515
Mexico — 459,287
Italy — 455,315
Germany — 412,202
United Kingdom — 339,570
Irish Free State (1922) — 211,234

When World War I broke out in Europe in 1914, every ship crossing the Atlantic was in danger, and immigration declined drastically. Though President Woodrow Wilson asked Americans to be neutral in the conflict, many took sides anyway. Often, immigrants sympathized with their home countries. Some favored the Allies — Great Britain, France, Russia, and Italy. Others supported the opposing side, the Central Powers — Germany, Austria-Hungary, and Turkey. Many Eastern Europeans — such as Poles, Czechs, Slovaks, Croats, and Slovenes — backed the Allies. They resented the treatment they had received as minorities in the Austro-Hungarian Empire.

THE UNITED STATES ENTERS THE WAR

In 1917 the United States declared war against the Central Powers. As in the Civil War, fighting in the American army was a demonstration of immigrant loyalty. In 1918 Congress rewarded the soldiers by extending the right of citizenship, regardless of race, to anyone who

Before the United States entered the war in 1917, Belgian immigrants in Massachusetts raised funds for Belgian refugees.

enlisted and served in the armed forces.

Poles, Czechs, Albanians, and other Slavs hoped that an Allied victory would result in independence for their native lands. The Fourteen Points that Wilson proposed as the terms of a peace agreement included a demand for self-determination (the right to choose their own government) for the peoples of Europe. Such idealistic promises increased immigrant support for Wilson's policies.

The war intensified Americanization efforts. The Interior Department developed educational programs for immigrants and a new Division of Immigrant Education was created. Some politicians began to refer to immigrants as "hyphenated Americans." Thus, for example, Italian-Americans or German-Americans" were not considered fully American.

Anti-German hysteria spread throughout the country. German aliens, who had been identified as a possible threat, were rounded up and held in confinement at Ellis Island. Anything that had any tinge of German influence had to be changed. Sauerkraut was renamed Liberty Cabbage, frankfurters became hot dogs. Even the German language became un-American. In Montana, all German books were removed from the libraries. South Dakota banned the speaking of German even on the telephone or in meetings of three or more people.

The antiforeign feeling encouraged Congress to pass the Immigration Act of 1917. It required a literacy test for immigrants. Each immigrant had to be able to read simple passages in their own language. The Act also established an Asiatic Barred Zone that included India, much of the rest of Asia, and the Pacific Islands. The new law resulted in a nearly complete ban on immigrant workers from Asia. The only Asians free to immigrate were the Filipinos, because their country was now a territory of the United States, as a result of the Spanish-American War of 1898.

The Armenian Genocide

Christian Armenians were targets of persecution by the Muslim Turks of the Ottoman Empire. Waves of persecution sent many Armenians to America seeking safety and a new home. They settled as farmers in the central valley farms and vineyards of California, as well as workers in mill towns in the Northeast.

In 1915, during World War I, the Turkish government claimed its Armenian citizens were a security risk because they supported Russia. As part of a program of genocide, two thirds of the Armenian people were either killed, deported, or sent into the Syrian desert to starve. Many of the survivors came to the United States. Jeanne, Molly, and Miriam Assidian, who arrived in the United States in 1922, were survivors. Miriam described their ordeal in Turkey:

"We . . . went into a Catholic church, which was full of Armenians. There was hardly any room to move around. The Turks had surrounded this church, and they were starting to pour kerosene all over and set it on fire. But fortunately, an American missionary came by, and . . . the Turks didn't light the fire, although you could hear screams coming from outside."

Victory Liberty Loan

This World War I poster asks for unity and contributions to the war effort. The names represent many of the nationalities that were now a part of the United States citizenry. Immigrants had family members on both sides of the war.

A New Nativism

During the war, revolution had broken out in Russia, and the Communist party took power. Refugees from the 1917 Russian Revolution fled to the United States. Russia's loss would be the United States' gain. Talented immigrants like George Balanchine, a ballet choreographer; musicians such as Sergei Rachmaninoff, and Igor Stravinsky; Vladimir Zworkyin, the inventor of television; and Igor Sikorsky, who invented the helicopter, enriched their adopted country.

To some Americans, the Russian Revolution was part of a worldwide radical movement. In 1919 a Wall Street explosion killed several people; many believed that the bomb had been planted by a foreigner. That same year strikes by labor unions involved one out of every five workers. Because many immigrants were involved in the labor movement, some Americans felt that these strikes were part of a plot to weaken the country.

As a result, a new spirit of "nativism," or antiforeign sentiment, arose in the 1920s. U.S. Attorney General A. Mitchell Palmer ordered the arrest of thousands of radicals and union leaders. Six hundred immigrants were deported. A resurgent Ku Klux Klan in the Midwest targeted immigrants, particularly Catholics and Jews.

Restricting Immigration

This ill-feeling toward foreigners led to louder calls for restricting immigration. In 1921 Congress passed the First National Origins Act. It introduced the idea of quotas by national origins — setting a certain number of immigrants for each country. These annual quotas, or limits, were set at 3 percent of the group living in the United States in 1910. This meant that groups like Germans, Irish, and English — which

The cartoon shows an anti-immigrant view with Uncle Sam being flooded.

THE FLOOD OF IMMIGRATION

JOHNSON'S IMMIGRATION MEASURES

"QUICK TURN IT OFF WITH THIS!"

were already heavily represented in the United States — had much higher quotas than those groups that had been coming for only a short time. The quota system would remain in force until 1965.

Many kinds of immigrants were exempt from the quota system. These included all immigrants from the Western Hemisphere. Actors, artists, singers, nurses, professors, domestic servants, and "aliens belonging to any recognized learned profession" were allowed in on a nonquota basis.

In 1924 Congress passed the Johnson-Reed Act. It cut the annual overall number of immigrants to 150,000 and reduced the national quotas to 2 percent of the number of each country's immigrants in 1890. An amendment changed the quotas to the number of people counted in the census of 1920. The Act, however, did not go into effect until 1929.

One provision of the 1924 act required potential immigrants to acquire a visa in their home country. To do so, they had to visit an American consulate and pass a physical and mental screening. Previously, this checkup had been the responsibility of the shipping companies. Josephine Cassidy, from Ireland, recalled that her sister was rejected when she tried to join her parents, who had emigrated earlier: "My mother worked very hard here in America to bring us over. She went according to age and brought my brother first. Supposedly my sister Lila was next. But when she went to the consul down in Queenstown, they rejected her because she had a swollen jaw. I had to take her place and I came on her passage. They transferred her name to me."

Dracula Enters the United States as an Illegal Alien

Bela Lugosi, who would star in many Hollywood horror pictures, jumped ship as an illegal immigrant when he arrived in October 1920. He turned himself in at Ellis Island in March 1921. He was allowed to stay after turning himself in because he gave his country of birth as Romania, so his being on a Hungarian police list as a radical would not keep him out of the country. A sample of his interrogation:

Name? — Bela Lugosi.
Age? — Thirty-eight.
Marital status? — Single.
Are you able to read? — Yes.
What language? — Roumanian.
How much money is in your possession? — $100.00.
Do you intend to become a U.S. citizen? — Yes.
Have you ever been in prison or almshouse, insane asylum or supported by charity? — No.
Are you a polygamist? — No.
Are you an anarchist? — No.
Do you believe in or advocate the overthrow by force of the U.S. government? — No.
Have you come to the United States because of solicitation or offer of employment? — No.
What is your condition of health — mental or physical? — Good.
Are you deformed or crippled? — No.
Complexion? — Dark.
Color of hair? — Brown.
Color of eyes? — Black.

THE GREAT MIGRATION

These newsboys proudly pose in front of an African-American newspaper office. Moving north usually meant a better life for these Americans.

In the past, there was little pull for African Americans to come north because employers didn't hire them. Immigrants held most of the unskilled jobs in the northern cities. When war began in Europe in 1914, immigration was cut off and the situation changed. Factory orders from European countries soared, while thousands of American workers left their jobs to go into the armed forces. The factory gates opened to African-American southerners. For people used to picking one hundred pounds of cotton for a dollar, factory work looked easy. In 1919 a factory employee in Chicago could get forty-eight cents an hour.

At the same time, the majority of African Americans lived in the southern states, where they experienced prejudice and discrimination. African Americans were deprived of the right to vote and lived under a humiliating system of segregation, called "Jim Crow." Most barely eked out a living farming small plots of land. "The reason why I want to come north," said a Georgia laborer, "is that the people don't pay enough for the labor that a man can do down here."

African Americans migrated north, making the same calculations and decisions that immigrants had made when coming to the United States. They would exchange a rural life of poverty and oppression for the city and a chance at a good job. Their immigration to this country had been in chains. Their migration north would be voluntary.

The migrants had several destinations. The most popular was Chicago, the end point of the Illinois Central Railroad, which came up from the Mississippi Delta region. Migrants settled on the South Side of Chicago, which became known as the "Black Metropolis," stretching more than thirty blocks. Detroit pulled migrants to the auto factories, where Henry Ford

Escaping the South

Mildred Arnold was part of the Great Migration. She came to Newark, New Jersey, from the South in 1924 when she was ten years old. The first leg of her journey was from the small town of North, South Carolina, to the city of Columbia, where a train could take her north. At the time, southern communities often tried to prevent African Americans from leaving so they would not lose their cheap labor.

"My daddy had to leave North at night. He had to get somebody with a horse and buggy to drive him to Columbia. But the next morning the man who drove him had to be back so they wouldn't know what [he] did that night. He had to be back the next morning to go to work just like he hadn't been anyplace.

"[Several months later my daddy] sent my mother some money and she got us all ready. It was just before the Fourth of July holiday. . . . There was a lady in Columbia who was like the underground railroad, like things you read about. Her place was a stopping off place. . . . When you got to Columbia, you could lay over at her place until you could get out; she would put you up.

"So my mother came up to the station that Saturday morning; we were all dressed. Not too much baggage. The baggage was gone; our clothes were gone. They were taken the night before. . . . We had just enough like we were going up to Columbia just for the day.

"We children were on the platform; I was the oldest. We didn't talk to anyone because you didn't want to let the white people know what was going on. You didn't dare. All my mother wanted to do was to get that train so she could get to Columbia. So we had to be very quiet. . . .

"[Finally the family reached New York City.] "My father and uncle met us at the Pennsylvania Railroad Station and brought us up here to Newton Street [in Newark, New Jersey], right across from the Newton Street School. We came on the trolley. . . . Oh Lord, to come up South Orange Avenue on that trolley car, that was something. I never rode on a trolley before; I had never even seen a trolley. I was saying to myself, 'What is this? We can ride like this?'. . . Everything was amazing. . . . You had a lot of gaslights in Newark. When they came on in the nighttime . . . the streets lit up. We had never seen anything like that. Down South, when the sun went down there was only darkness."

was paying top dollar for workers, regardless of race. The steel mills of Pittsburgh, Cleveland, and Gary, Indiana, created other destinations. Then there was New York City, where a new African-American neighborhood named Harlem was growing.

Between 1910 and 1930 more than 1.5 million African Americans moved to cities in the north and west. It was a process that by 1960 would bring 6 million people from the South — the largest internal migration in our nation's history. It became known as the Great Migration.

The Chicago railroad station was the Ellis Island for African Americans going north — the starting place of a new life.

During the 1920s, for the first time, the greatest number of immigrants came from Canada — about 1 million people. Many who arrived during the 1920s were French speakers, coming to work in the mills and other factories in New England. In 1920, 73 percent of the French Canadians in the United States lived in that part of the country. Some were actually Europeans trying to beat the quota system by going to Canada first. There was no quota for immigrants from Canada or Mexico, but a person had to live there for five years before immigrating to the United States.

Mining was one of the main occupations of Mexican immigrants like these working in Arizona around 1910.

MEXICAN IMMIGRATION GROWS

To the Mexicans, the United States was "El Norte," the North. As word of the better opportunities spread, immigration fever began. News of the success of fellow villagers encouraged others. Returning Mexicans wore shoes and flaunted their wealth. Jesus Garcia, who later immigrated, remembered: "As I heard a lot about the United States, it was my dream to come here." Mexican field-workers were making twelve cents a day at home while the daily wages in the Southwest for similar work ranged from one dollar to three dollars and fifty cents.

El Paso, Texas, sometimes called the Mexican Ellis Island, was the most important border entry for Mexicans. The Stanton Street Bridge linked El Paso to Ciudad Juarez, and all one had to do was walk across it. But the reception on the other side was often terrifying. First, the immigrants had to undergo the humiliation of a public bath and give the officials their clothing for fumigation. They were herded into examination pens, where up to 600 people had to wait for hours with no drinking fountains or toilet facilities. The passage of the Immigration Act of 1917 had added a literacy test and a "head tax" as entry requirements. These conditions were usually applied only to poor immigrants. Those who dressed well or showed they were upper class often could forego the tests as well as the public bath.

The Mexican Revolution, which began in 1910 and continued for almost ten years, sent refugees pouring across the border. They came to the Southwest, particularly California, where commercial agriculture was booming. Large land reclamation and irrigation projects brought water to land that previously could not be farmed. At the same time, the new restrictions on Asian immigration had made agricultural workers scarce. So the growers started to send recruiting agents to Mexico.

Mexicans worked in berry fields from February through June, and then picked grapes and cotton. Rosaura Valdez described the difficul-

Mexican refugees crossing the Rio Grande. Once the Mexican Revolution broke out in 1910, the number of refugees increased.

ties of cotton-picking: "I'd have a twelve-foot sack, about this wide. I'd tie the sack around my waist and the sack would go between my legs and I'd go on the cotton row, picking cotton and just putting it in there. . . . So when we finally got it filled real good then we would pick up the sack, toss it up on our shoulders, and then I would walk, put it up there on the scale and have it weighed, put it back on my

French Canadians came to all the northern states. In New England they were important in the dangerous logging work.

These immigrants from Guadeloupe in the Caribbean came through Ellis Island in 1911.

shoulder, climb up a ladder on a wagon, and empty that sack in."

Mexicans were moving outside the Southwest as well. By the end of the 1920s, Mexican immigrants were picking beets in Minnesota, assembling cars in Detroit, packing fish in Alaska, laying track in Kansas, and meatpacking in Chicago. Still, 80 percent of the Mexican-American population lived in the traditional states of California, Colorado, Texas, New Mexico, and Arizona.

CARIBBEANS ARRIVE

The Caribbean also sent many immigrants to the United States during these years. Many Caribbean-born arrivals settled in Harlem, the capital of Black America. They mixed with African Americans from New York and African Americans who had migrated from the South. "Harlem became the symbol of liberty and the Promised Land to Negroes everywhere," wrote Adam Clayton Powell, Sr., about the neighborhood in the 1920s. This was the time of the Harlem Renaissance, a flowering of African-American art and literature, and Caribbeans played an important part in it. Caribbean-born blacks were often successful in business as well. The most famous Jamaican immigrant was Marcus Garvey, who started the Back-to-Africa movement, the largest African-American organization in the nation's history.

The twenties saw the beginning of the Puerto Rican colony in New York. It started in World War I and grew to 135,000 before the massive migration of the 1940s. Actually,

The Runaway Vacuum Cleaner

Roberto Vallangca came from the Philippines in 1927 when he was twenty and ambitious for education. He described his first work experience as a houseboy in San Jose, California:

"She [the woman of the house] told me to go to the garage to get the broom. I could not find the garage so she showed me where it was. I swept the garage and the stairway, piled all the rubbish in one corner and even swept under the trees in the yard. When she came down in an hour or two, she smiled and said that I did a good job but that I need not have swept under the trees. . . .

"We went half-way down the hall and she opened a closet, telling me to bring the vacuum cleaner with me, at the same time pointing to it. I had never seen one before but I picked it up and carried it on my shoulder as I was used to carrying large things while in the Philippines. When I reached the living room, she said, 'Roberto, I want you to vacuum the living room.' I was afraid to tell the lady that I did not know about a vacuum cleaner, either. So all I said was, 'Yes, ma'am.' I was sizing up the vacuum cleaner when she looked at me, saying, 'Go on, take the cord and plug it in that socket there,' pointing to the wall. . . .

"I plugged the cord into the wall but nothing happened. I fooled around with it, turned it around, upside down, touched and felt around the base but nothing happened. Then I saw that the plug was pulled out of the wall socket. So I plugged it in again. Suddenly the vacuum motor roared and the machine started toward me. I jumped up with fright and ran to the door.

"'Roberto,' she said, 'You are really ignorant — what am I going to do with you?' I felt so bad and was so embarrassed that I could not speak. Then she said, 'Listen, Roberto, and watch carefully, I will show you what to do.' Then she showed me how to plug the cord in the wall, put on the switch and she ran the vacuum cleaner along the carpet, telling me to move the chairs carefully as I went along. Then she relinquished the vacuum cleaner to me — my first lesson having been completed. I was now a seasoned houseboy — well almost!"

New York was the second colony of Puerto Ricans outside their home island. The first had been in Hawaii, whose plantation owners sent agents to Puerto Rico to recruit sugarcane cutters.

The first Filipino immigrants were the war brides of American soldiers who fought in the Spanish-American War of 1898. Then, a small number of Filipinos came to the mainland as students. Prejudice forced them into migrant farmwork, particularly in California. In June, many went north to Alaska to work in the annual salmon harvest. Men with college degrees worked cleaning, processing, and canning the fish. They lived in segregated wooden barracks away from white workers, and received lower pay for the same jobs.

CHAPTER TEN

IMMIGRANTS AT A TRICKLE

Christos Spanos came to the United States from Cyprus in 1930 at nineteen. The United States was then in the depths of hard times.

"My older brother had somebody meet us. He lived in Manhattan on West Forty-fourth Street. It was like a Greek colony there. . . .

"It was the Depression. There were bread lines out in the street. There was a bread line in Times Square. . . . There was a bread line or soup line everywhere. Stores went out of business. Men sold apples, five cents an apple on the street. . . .

"Luckily, I got a job right away. I went to the employment agency on Sixth Avenue. . . .

"'Ever been a busboy?'

"'Sure,' I lied.

"'Good. It pays sixteen dollars. You work twelve hours a day, seven days a week. It's called Excelsior Cafeteria at Yankee Stadium. You go there.'

"'Sixteen dollars a day?'

"'No, sixteen dollars a week, and you've got to pay my fee in advance.'

"'How can I pay in advance? I don't have any money. That's why I'm looking for a job.'

"'Fine, you can pay me when you get paid, providing you get me Babe Ruth's autograph. He takes his coffee at the Excelsior.'"

Spanos was lucky to find a job at all. During the Great Depression, one quarter of the working population was unemployed. People lost their homes, farms, and businesses. The Depression, which began with the stock market crash of 1929, ended only after the United States entered World War II, a time of trial at home and abroad.

During the Depression and war years, immigration declined. World War II increased people's pride in being American, as seen in this Italian couple's toast to the New Year in New York's Little Italy.

During the Great Depression, the country struggled with unemployment and poverty. Louis Nana, a tool- and die-maker from Italy, remembered, "When the Depression came, first one half of the factory was laid off and then the other half. I was one of the last." For the first time his wife had to work. "We got by because Edna went to work. That's the only time I had her work. She worked in a laundry; she didn't make much but it helped out a little bit."

In 1929 the Johnson-Reed Act went into effect, severely limiting new immigration. In the early 1930s, for the first time ever, more immigrants were leaving the United States than arriving. In 1931 immigration fell below 100,000 for the first time since the Civil War. Nearly two thirds of the allowed quota went unfulfilled.

The Depression hit hard in the steel-making city of Pittsburgh, and many immigrants lost their jobs.

THE NEW DEAL

In 1933 Franklin D. Roosevelt was elected president. He proposed social programs, called the New Deal, designed to stimulate the economy and provide jobs for the unemployed. Some New Deal programs were available only to citizens. With jobs scarce, many employers felt they should favor citizens over noncitizens. As a result, many immigrants became naturalized citizens.

The Roosevelt administration looked kindly on unionization as well. For the first time, the federal government recognized the right of workers to organize. Immigrants in the labor movement felt that they were more fully accepted in American life. In the newly formed Congress of Industrial Organizations (CIO), immigrants played important roles.

Who Was Coming

1931–1940
528,431 immigrants.
Germany — 114,058,
Canada — 108,527;
Italy — 68,028

1941–1950
1,035,039 immigrants.
Germany — 226,578;
Canada — 171,718;
United Kingdom —
139,306

1951–1960
2,515,479 immigrants.
Germany — 477,765;
Canada — 377,952;
Mexico — 299,811;
United Kingdom —
202,824

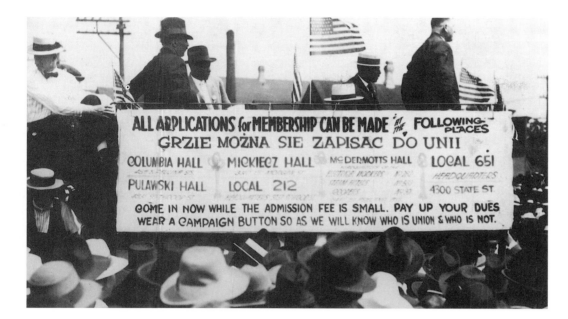

ALL APPLICATIONS for MEMBERSHIP CAN BE MADE at the FOLLOWING PLACES
GRZIE MOŻNA SIE ZAPISAC DO UNII
COLUMBIA HALL • MICKIECZ HALL • McDERMOTTS HALL • LOCAL 651
PULAWSKI HALL • LOCAL 212 • HEADQUARTERS 4300 STATE ST.
COME IN NOW WHILE THE ADMISSION FEE IS SMALL. PAY UP YOUR DUES
WEAR A CAMPAIGN BUTTON SO AS WE WILL KNOW WHO IS UNION & WHO IS NOT.

During the Depression, labor unions became more powerful. Poles led the unionization of meat packers in Chicago.

Hard times encouraged people to cooperate and support one another. Both Filipinos and Mexicans were among the largest groups of agricultural workers in the West. But they had not been able to work together to demand higher wages and better working conditions. In 1936 a farmworker group called the Filipino Labor Union organized a strike. Mexican laborers joined the fight. The strikers received a charter from the American Federation of Labor, which had previously turned its back on agricultural workers.

Such activities angered some whites who were in favor of excluding all nonwhite immigrants. They pressured Congress to pass the Tydings-McDuffie Act of 1934, which promised independence to the Philippines by 1946. Filipinos were reclassified as aliens — and as nonwhites, they were barred from becoming citizens. Only fifty Filipinos a year were permitted to immigrate to the mainland United States. Congress even offered to pay the passage back to the Philippines for those willing to return. Fewer than 5 percent took up the offer.

Mexicans were also victims of anti-immigrant hysteria. The government responded to this prejudice with massive deportations. During the 1930s about 500,000 Mexicans were forcibly deported. Many of them were American citizens.

A small number of Mexicans came in the 1930s, like these women at the U.S. Immigration station at El Paso.

The Golden Exiles

During the 1930s, the door to America did open a bit for a few select immigrants of high achievement. A loophole in the 1924 law permitted visas above the quotas for "teachers of higher education." This made it possible for many of Europe's finest scientists, artists, and intellectuals to immigrate. So talented were they in all fields that they are known as the Golden Exiles.

These exiles would help make the United States the world leader in arts and sciences. In 1933 Albert Einstein, the greatest scientist of the twentieth century, came to the United States from Germany. From Hungary came John von Neumann, the greatest mathematician of his time, as well as atomic scientists Edward Teller and Leo Szilard. Poles contributed Stanislaus Ulam, a mathematician who helped develop nuclear weapons. Others who arrived in the prewar years were German artists and architects like George Grosz, Joseph Albers, Marcel Breuer, Hans Hofman, Walter Gropius, and Lotte Lenya. From Italy came scientist Enrico Fermi and his wife Laura, musician Arturo Toscanini, and many others.

During the 1930s, trouble and disaster stalked the world. In 1933 Adolf Hitler and his Nazi party came to power in Germany. Almost at once, Hitler instituted a policy of ruthless persecution against Jews. The Nazis purged Jews from universities, scientific institutions, and even its Olympic sports team.

Albert Einstein was the most famous German Jewish immigrant of the 1930s.

As the situation worsened, and Jews tried desperately to leave Europe, they found the American immigration quotas filled. In the quota system of the 1920s, there was no separate category for refugees. Instead of following its traditional policy of providing a haven for the downtrodden, the United States government and people chose to turn back the refugees.

Americans were edgy about foreigners. In 1940 the Alien Registration Act required all aliens to register with the government, filling out a form about their activities. Failure to register was a deportable act.

THE UNITED STATES GOES TO WAR

On December 7, 1941, Japan attacked Pearl Harbor in Hawaii. The next day, the United States declared war on Japan and entered World War II. Only hours after Pearl Harbor, the FBI activated its "dangerous aliens" list and took into custody leaders of the German-American and Italian-American communities. Hundreds of them were interned at Ellis Island. On the West Coast, others were picked up and after short hearings sent to an internment camp at Fort Missoula, Montana. Filippo Moninari of San Jose, California, remembered that he wasn't even given a chance to put on shoes and had to wear slippers in the cold Montana weather.

During the war, China was an ally of the United States, and

The FBI Breaks into a Japanese Home

George Akimoto from California remembered the day when the FBI came for his father, a Japanese immigrant, after the attack on Pearl Harbor in 1941:

"My dad was head of a couple of organizations which I guess the F.B.I. considered dangerous or subversive. So one morning, about 7 o'clock, they broke through our front door and came in with sub-machine guns. . . . They saw my sea scout uniform and said, 'What's that?'

"I said, 'Can't you see the boy scout emblem on that?'

"They questioned us, and then they said, 'We're going to have to take him.' They took my mother's knitting book that was written in Japanese — you know, knit one, purl two. They thought it was a code book. That was the only evidence they took when they took my old man.

I could see them just running that thing through the army deciphering machine!

"So they took him and put him in the local jail. This was in the wintertime. He didn't even take his topcoat because he thought he would be back in a day or two. Next thing we know, we got a letter from Bismarck, North Dakota. He's up there in a camp freezing his butt off in the snow up there without his topcoat! Eventually he wound up in Santa Fe, New Mexico, actually with prisoners of war from the European theater — Germans, Italians. Then all of a sudden, they released him and he came back to Arkansas where we were [in a relocation camp]."

the prejudice against Chinese lessened. In 1943 Congress passed a law allowing Chinese to immigrate to the United States. The yearly quota was only 102 people, which included Chinese from any part of the world. In addition, Congress allowed Chinese immigrants to become naturalized American citizens.

With numbered tags around their necks, the Mochida family waits for the evacuation bus.

INTERNMENT OF JAPANESE AMERICANS

Immediately after Pearl Harbor, hundreds of Japanese living on the West Coast were rounded up by the FBI. These included such leaders of the community as language teachers, Shinto and Buddhist priests and nuns, and journalists on Japanese-language newspapers. Those who worked for the state, local, or federal governments were fired from their jobs.

On February 19, 1942, President Roosevelt issued Executive Order 9066, which authorized the evacuation

and internment of Japanese Americans. There was no distinction made between Japanese immigrants and those Japanese who were born in this country and thus citizens. Soon, all Americans of Japanese descent were prohibited from living, working, or traveling on the West Coast. Families were given little more than a week to get ready to move. They had to sell their homes and shops (which often went for prices far below what they were worth), and could take only what they could carry. They were packed into buses and trains with the windows covered and carried to collection points such as racetracks and fairgrounds. Some lived in filthy horse stalls. Then they were sent to internment camps in desolate and isolated parts of the country in California, Idaho, Wyoming, Utah, Arizona, Colorado, and Arkansas.

SERVING IN THE MILITARY

Many Asian Americans, both immigrant and native-born, rushed to serve in the United States military forces to show their patriotism. Foreign-born soldiers who served in the American armed forces could become naturalized citizens. This was still virtually the only way for Asians to gain this right.

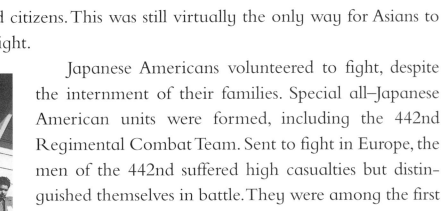

Japanese Americans volunteered to fight, despite the internment of their families. Special all–Japanese American units were formed, including the 442nd Regimental Combat Team. Sent to fight in Europe, the men of the 442nd suffered high casualties but distinguished themselves in battle. They were among the first to liberate the concentration camp at Dachau. The 442nd Combat Team received more medals for bravery than any unit of its size in American military history.

FINDING WORKERS

The war brought a labor shortage at home, particularly in agriculture. The United States reversed its policy toward Mexican immigrants. In the Depression, it had deported them. Now, starting in 1943, the government imported agricultural workers

Mexican laborers arrive to harvest beets in Stockton, California, in 1943. They were needed because U.S. farmworkers had gone to fight in World War II.

A Death-Camp Survivor

Tilly Stimler survived the Holocaust and came to the United States. Born in Romania in 1930, she lost her whole family — parents, brother, and sister — in concentration camps. She described the terror of her experience as a girl:

"My father was taken first [in 1944]. . . . Later the rest of us were taken to Auschwitz. We traveled for six days to reach there. I can't explain to you how it looked when we saw it. I think hell will never scare me. We saw the smoke and the Germans, people dressed in leather coats. . . .

"As we came off the train, we were told to just go. Then, as I started to go with my mother and my two sisters, we were told to leave everything there. Later my mother and my oldest sister went back to get some things, and I've never seen them again. . . .

"We were taken to these barracks and all of our clothes were taken off and our hair was shaved off. We looked like we weren't normal. We didn't know what was going on. We were told that we couldn't say anything, couldn't talk to a German.

"The biggest impression I have of that day is that it was raining, pouring rain. In May it's still very cold in Europe and especially in Poland. You remember your mother always saying, 'Don't go out in the cold and rain; you'll catch cold.' Here we were with our shaved heads and in short sleeves, standing in the pouring rain. I remember thinking, 'Don't the Germans realize I'll catch cold?' . . .

"Finally we reached Bergen-Belsen.

"Bergen-Belsen, as I said, was one of the worst camps. People were dying of disease and hunger everywhere. You just stepped over dead people. . . . Now the last days at Bergen-Belsen were unbelievable. Just before liberation the Germans brought in more people from the other camps. As I was bringing them in, I saw three girls from my hometown and I called to one of them. I told her whose child I was and she said, 'Oh My God. That's you.' I told her I was very weak but she made me get up.

"She said, 'Don't worry, it could just be a matter of hours. Don't you hear the shooting? You know what's going on? We could be liberated tonight.' And so she and her friends helped to get me up. I was so weak. But seeing them gave me some kind of moral support. And so they were right. The next day the British arrived and liberated us.

"But the Germans had poisoned the bread so we didn't have bread for a few days. Even after we were liberated, many died. Although the British tried to help us, they just didn't have enough doctors and trained people. We hadn't eaten for such a long time, and were so hungry."

from all over Latin America. This effort was called the Bracero Program (*bracero* means "day laborer" in Spanish).

Agreements were made with the governments of British Honduras (now Belize), Jamaica, Barbados, the British West Indies, and Mexico to send contract laborers to the United States. About a half million workers participated in the harvesting of crops. In the case of Mexican workers, the program was extended until 1964.

The defeat of Germany and Japan left the United States far and away the strongest power in the world. Never had the riches and opportunities of the United States appeared more alluring. "The understanding of people outside the United States is that it's the country of opportunity," remembered Ulumdsha Albataew, a Mongolian Buddhist who fled the Soviet Union after the war. "If anybody wants to move to some other country, the United States is the first country that they want to go to."

DISPLACED PERSONS

At the end of the war, millions of refugees were stranded throughout Europe and Asia. Some had no nationality they could call their own. Others were the survivors of Hitler's death camps, and they no longer wished to live in Germany. Many Eastern Europeans did not want to return to countries that were now under the influence of the Soviet Union. These refugees, called Displaced Persons or DPs, lived in camps mainly in Austria and Germany, waiting for some country to accept them.

Charles Simic, who came to the United States from Yugoslavia after waiting nine years, remembered vividly how he felt about being a DP. "'Displaced Persons' is the name they had for us back in 1945, and that's what we truly were. . . . We were the starving refugees, hundreds of thousands of them in trains, camps, and prisons, dipping stale bread into water soup, searching for lice on their children's heads and squawking in dozens of languages about their awful fate. . . ."

Refugees had to find an individual or organization to sponsor them. Often the sponsor would be a relative or friend, but sometimes, he or she was a complete stranger. Tiiu Lapsins and her family from Estonia were sponsored by a farmer in

These Chinese war brides dined as the guests of the Portland, Oregon, Chinese Womens Club.

A War Bride from Italy

*Elda Torini came to America on a Pan Am airliner from Italy in 1947 when she was twenty.
She was engaged to an American soldier who had served in Sicily.*

"I flew from Rome to Lisbon to New York. . . . There were fifty girls coming here, all on the same plane. All a similar age. Going to marry or meet their boyfriends who were soldiers or in the navy. . . . We landed at La Guardia. One of the girls was met by her boyfriend, and he gave her a mink coat. I thought, 'Wow! A mink coat!' . . .

"Then I was taken with all those girls to Ellis Island, but we didn't know where we was going to end up. We started crying. We got in the ferry. Suitcase, all ripped up, three days being up and down. We carry everything, and got to this place. And there was a big, big room with all the beds and they say, 'This your bed, this your bed.' Oh, my God, we started to cry. . . . In the morning, a breakfast like I never saw in my life. The dining room was full of all kinds of foods. Pancakes, French toast. . . .

"So I was sitting there reading a book when that lady says, 'Elda Torini.' I says, 'Yeah!' I'm screaming. 'We got good news for you. Your boyfriend is coming. . . . The ferry leaves at three o'clock. But when you get there, don't move. Stay with everybody else . . .'

"When I got off the ferry, I spotted him. And it was snowing, it was freezing. I had never seen snow in my life. And I was wearing a spring coat and high heels. I didn't find no boyfriend to bring me a mink coat. But when I saw him, I says, 'I don't care,' and I broke away and ran in the snow to him. . . . A few days later, January 12, 1948, we were married."

North Carolina who expected them to work. "In North Carolina they didn't know what an Estonian was. . . . [The farmer showed] my father . . . a couple of broken-down tractors, and he asked my father, 'Do you know what they are? What they are used for?' Of course, they didn't work. My father had to work there with horses and plows."

In 1948 Congress passed the Displaced Persons Act, which helped people to enter the United States even when their quota had been filled. They could "mortgage" future quotas. In other words, the quota in future years would be reduced so that these people could come in at the present time. Between 1948 and 1952, about 400,000 people were admitted under these provisions.

A group of European arrivals after the war looks out on New York harbor with the same hopes and dreams as immigrants before and after.

EASING ENTRY

Congress also recognized the special case of war brides — foreign women who had married American servicemen. It exempted them from the provisions of the immigration acts, allowing them to come to America with their husbands. The war-bride exemption was particu-

Many Puerto Rican immigrants found jobs in the garment trade. But the industry was starting to decline by the 1950s.

larly helpful to Asian women, who in the past had had a difficult time entering the United States. Because the United States kept occupation forces in Japan for years after the war, many American soldiers met and married Japanese women. An estimated 200,000 Asian war brides immigrated to the United States between 1945 and 1952.

Asian immigrants were no longer excluded from becoming naturalized citizens. In 1946 Congress passed the Luce-Cellar Act, which allowed the naturalization of people from India and gave them a quota of 105 immigrants per year. That same year Congress declared the Philippines independent, set an annual quota of 100 Filipino immigrants, and made them eligible to become citizens, too. In 1952 Japanese and Koreans were granted the same rights.

THE FIRST AIRBORNE MIGRATION

The largest numbers of newcomers to the continental United States in the 1940s were from other nations of the Americas. In 1946 hundreds of thousands of Puerto Ricans started to leave their Caribbean homeland in what has been called "the greatest airborne migration in history."

Many Puerto Ricans had worked in the sugar fields of large plantations for low wages. Better jobs and opportunities beckoned on the mainland. Because Puerto Rico was an American territory, its people were United States citizens and didn't need visas or resident alien cards. Despite this, many mainland Americans regarded them as foreigners because they spoke Spanish.

Maria Rosario, one of twelve children, came from Puerto Rico when she was fourteen. She remembered how difficult it was for her at first in a mainland school. "The teachers, however, were very good. Some were Spanish teachers. Bilingual. They helped me. They put me in bilingual classes. I had some classes in Spanish to help me in English. After a while, they put me in an English-speaking class."

By 1960 there were more than 1 million Puerto Ricans on the mainland — almost as many as on the island. Many settled in El Barrio in northern Manhattan. They found work in hotels, nightclubs, restaurants, and sweatshops, as well as in the meatpacking and taxi industries. There were also Puerto Rican communities in Chicago, Philadelphia, and parts of Indiana and Ohio.

The Cubans started arriving in large numbers when Fidel Castro came to power in 1959. The early arrivals tended to be rich and well educated.

COLD WAR REFUGEES

At the end of World War II, tension arose between the United States and its former ally, the Soviet Union. The Soviets took control of many of the nations of Eastern Europe. American attempts to block the spread of communism resulted in what was called the Cold War. Refugees from Communist countries sometimes were able to reach the United States, and this time they were not turned back.

The Cold War spread when the Communists won a civil war and established the People's Republic of China in 1949. Though the United States exchanged ambassadors with the Soviet Union, it refused to recognize the People's Republic as the government of China. In 1953 the United States allowed more than 25,000 Chinese refugees to immigrate, giving them permanent resident status.

The Cold War made Americans sympathetic to the Hungarian refugees of 1956. In that year Hungarians challenged the Soviet Union's domination of their country. Soviet tanks swiftly put down the revolt. About 171,000 Hungarians escaped to Austria. More than 58,000 came to the United States, under the quota exemption permitted in the McCarran-Walter Act.

CUBAN EXILES

In 1959 Fidel Castro and a group of rebels overthrew the Cuban government. Castro's increasingly radical policies pushed many wealthy and highly educated Cubans into emigrating. The United States granted the Cubans automatic political asylum. Private relief agencies gave them help in resettling, for many had left their wealth in Cuba. In December 1960, President Eisenhower ordered a Cuban Refugee Center to be set up and federal funds to help the refugees.

The Cubans who fled to the United States did not think of themselves as immigrants. They thought they would stay in the United States only until Castro was overthrown. Gloria Ruiz-Mesa Graff, who came from Cuba with her parents in 1960, recalled: "In the beginning my parents really believed that we were going to be here for maybe just two or three years. . . . My father had a very good job [in Cuba.] He was a judge, and we had three homes. We were very comfortable and we liked it there. That was home, we wanted to go back."

This Greek wedding in Texas in the 1950s looks much like a wedding of any other group at the time.

Success on the Second Try

Marta Mishan escaped with her sister from Hungary after the October 1956 revolution. They went to Austria and from there by plane to the United States. She was only twelve and her sister was twenty.

"My sister and I attempted to cross the border twice. The first time we went with a group but we were caught [at the border] by the Russians. Earlier, when the revolution was happening, the border was open. But we didn't want to leave if the revolution was going to be successful. So we left after [it] had been put down, after the Russians came back into Budapest and took over Hungary. . . .

"We walked all night and ended up making a circle. There is a point at which Hungary, Austria and Czechoslovakia meet in a corner. This is the corner we went to. We went through Austria, Czechoslovakia, and back into Hungary, and right into the arms of the Russians. It was winter and we were really glad to be caught. . . . [The Russians] were very kind. They warmed us up; they had a tent at the border. In the early part of the morning they put us into a large group; they put us on a truck and took us to jail.

"The jails were very crowded, you understand, because of the revolution. There were more important criminals to hold than people like us, so after two or three days they transported us back to where we came from, hoping that we were not going to try again. . . .

"My sister wouldn't give up. She wanted to try again. This time we went with a small group, my sister and I and one more couple whom we didn't know. This time again we were caught but it was by [loyal] Hungarian patrol. . . . It turned out that the head of the patrol was my sister's high-school mate. He was very helpful. He showed us the way to get across the border. And we managed to get to Austria."

FROM IMMIGRANTS TO ETHNIC GROUPS

After World War II many returning veterans bought houses in the suburbs, away from the old immigrant neighborhoods where they or their parents had lived. Life in the suburbs was different from life in ethnic neighborhoods. The 1950s was a decade of conformity — people wanted to fit into the American ideal. The standard was a family in which the father worked and the mother stayed home to take care of the children. People shed the old immigrant traditions that had united the urban neighborhoods.

This Korean family, in their herbal shop in Los Angeles, shows the prosperity of the 1950s.

CHAPTER ELEVEN

COMING TO AMERICA TODAY

José Pacheco came to the United States from Mexico. He runs a company that encourages development of new technologies. José recalled:

"Up until I was seven I lived in Mexico City with my mother and my grandparents, in one of the poorest sections of the city.

"So it was quite a shock when one day my mother, Mercedes, asked me the question that would change the rest of my life: 'Would I like to go to live in Los Estados Unidos?' She was asking me to leave my friends, beloved grandparents, cousins, aunts and uncles, everything important to me, to go to a faraway land in search of something called a better life. I'm surprised she asked me at all, since I was but a child seven years old. She began then to teach me that my destiny was a choice.

"Until then, my grandparents had been like my parents and I like their child, but now this might change. I asked Mama la and Papa Chilo what I should do. Through a cascade of tears and love they simply said, 'Go and learn.'

"Was it their hope that I would learn how to read, as Mama la never had, or perhaps that I would finish elementary school as my mother had done, or attend university and become a doctor like my uncle? It was much simpler than that. I was to learn the lesson of how they lived their lives: 'Go and learn that within each human being, including you, lies extraordinary power to create and expand the limits of possibility. . . . And then learn the most important lesson: That this path requires responsibility to be more helpful to the world and those you love than you ever imagined you could be.'

"So it was that I tearfully said yes to my mother's question."

José Pacheco was one of millions of immigrants who have come since 1965. A change in the nation's law that year ushered in a new era of immigration. In the last decades of the twentieth century, the United States welcomed the largest number of immigrants in our history. Today our country has the largest foreign-born population in the world.

Throughout the 1970s, many Vietnamese fled their homes trying to find safety across the sea. These so-called boat people often met pirates and violence before they reached a safe haven in the United States.

A NEW APPROACH

By the 1960s it was apparent that the Johnson-Reed Act of 1924 was inadequate to handle the demand for immigration to this country. More than two thirds of the total quota slots were assigned to immigrants from just three countries — Germany, Great Britain, and Ireland. Many of these slots went unfilled, while people from other countries had to wait for years to be admitted.

President John F. Kennedy, in a 1963 speech, attacked the national origins quota system: "It neither satisfies a national need nor accomplishes an international purpose. In an age of interdependence among nations, such a system is an anachronism for it discriminates among applicants for admission into the United States on the basis of the accident of birth."

President Lyndon Johnson spoke out against those policies before signing the Immigration and Naturalization Act of 1965. "This system violates the basic principle of American democracy — the principle that values and rewards each man on the basis of his merit as a man. It has been un-American in the highest sense, because it has been untrue to the faith that brought thousands to these shores even before we were a country."

THE IMMIGRATION AND NATURALIZATION ACT

The new act scrapped the national origins criteria for admissions of immigrants. Visas would be granted on a first-come, first-served basis, with an eight-step preference system. Most of the preferences dealt with family unification or the needs of American employers for workers; one dealt with refugees. The Act assigned 170,000 visas a year to the countries of the Eastern Hemisphere, with a ceiling of 20,000 for any one country. And for the first time, the legislation established a ceiling of 120,000 for the Western Hemisphere. (The Act was amended in 1976 to set a ceiling of 20,000 per country in this hemisphere, too.) Over and above the total ceiling of 290,000 immigrants, the parents, spouses, and children of immigrants already in the United States could be admitted without limit.

The Romance of America

Shanti, an Indian immigrant, remembered how watching movies made her want to go to America.

"I wanted to go to America. Much of our cinema came from the United States. Life seemed so glamorous. My favorite American films were the romance movies. I thought men in America treated women very differently than the way men in India treated women. In the American movies, the men would always try to win the heart of a lady. Maybe it was because I was at that age when I started thinking of who my love will be when I am older. The women in these movies had so much control. They had many men to choose from. They were making decisions of which men they would want to marry. No one was making the decision for them."

The Congressional leaders who sponsored the 1965 Act thought that it would result only in a slight increase in immigrants. Politicians and population experts agreed that most of those who would take advantage of the new system would come from southern and eastern Europe. But by 1965 the effects of World War II were ending. Europe was becoming far more prosperous than it had been in the past. And the birthrate was falling, so population pressure was not a problem. Europeans were not as eager to come to the United States as they had been in the past.

Conditions were different in Asia, Africa, the Caribbean, the Middle East, and Latin America. Over-population, underdevelopment, and lack of opportunity were all push factors that sent a flood of immigrants from those areas to the United States after 1965.

That was not the only difference between post-1965 immigrants and those who came earlier. The proportion of women to men was high; some years women immigrants outnumbered men. There was also a higher percentage of professionals among the immigrants than in the past. These new immigrants were pulled to the United States by hopes for steady employment and higher pay. Many had been impressed by the American lifestyle as shown in movies and television. Their immigration would change their lives and transform the United States as well.

Yadira Betances (at right), from the Dominican Republic, receives an award along with newcomers from Vietnam and Italy in Lawrence, Massachusetts.

The 1965 Act allowed 6 percent of the total for refugees if necessary. Those coming with the hope of getting refugee status in the United States are called *asylees*. The fate of asylees is decided by United States officials after they arrive in the United States.

REFUGEES FROM SOUTHEAST ASIA

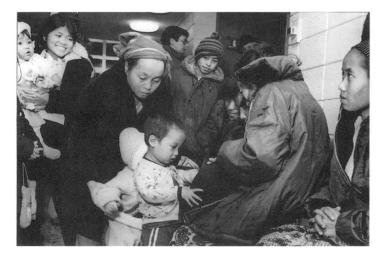

The Hmong of Laos supported the American side in the war in Southeast Asia. Afterward, many like this family escaped to the United States.

These Vietnamese boat people arrived in Malaysia, hoping to eventually reach the United States.

Refugees became more important to immigration policy as a result of American policies in Asia. The ten-year Vietnam War (1965–1975) led to the arrival of many refugees from Vietnam and the neighboring countries of Laos and Cambodia. With the defeat of the United States' ally South Vietnam in 1975, the first wave of 135,000 government officials and military personnel fled to American warships. The 1975 Indochina Migration Refugee Assistance Act gave American aid to help them start new lives.

A second wave of Southeast Asians fled persecution by the new Communist governments in the area. Some were "boat people" — refugees who fled across the South China Sea to neighboring countries. Some drowned or encountered pirates. Even those who arrived found

that the host countries didn't want them. In 1978 many Cambodians escaped the "killing fields" of their homeland. So, too, did refugees from Laos, particularly the Hmong, a minority group. Mayker Yang, a young Hmong girl, remembered: "We didn't take anything; just one or two clothes. We had to walk in the jungles, and it took us a long time, that's all I remember. Many days. I was still little. I asked my mother, when are we going to get there?"

Malaysia and Thailand set up camps where the refugees stayed until they could

From Vietnam to America

Mai Leu, the oldest of nine children of a Vietnamese forest ranger, started planning her trip to the United States in 1976. She fled with two brothers in 1978 by boat to Malaysia.

"We got to the boat at night. But before you come to the sea you must go on the river. This was very dangerous because at night it was difficult to tell the right direction. But about twelve A.M. we got to the sea and after that we were free.

"But on the way we met pirates. . . . We had a strong storm and we lost direction. We saw a boat [and] put up SOS flags. When they came near we saw Italian flags At first they were very nice. They gave us fresh water and some rice. But they waited until another boat came and then they took everything.

"After three days or four days and nights we got
to Malaysia and came to a refugee camp. Just temporary and very dirty with over one thousand people there. They had no bathrooms. Nothing. We stayed there for one week. After that they carried us to an island where there were over forty thousand people. No fresh water or nothing. No bathroom. You must go up the hill. We had to go swimming every day to bathe.

"We didn't have enough food; we were hungry all of the time. We stayed there for over six months. Finally we established contact with the Lutheran Church, and they agreed to sponsor us to come to the United States. We came here on July 29."

---

gain admittance to the United States. Many waited for years, because they needed an American sponsor. There were few Southeast Asian relatives living in the United States, so many church groups stepped forward to act as sponsors.

SOVIET JEWISH IMMIGRATION

European immigration declined after 1965 with the exception of Jews from the Soviet Union. During the Cold War, the Soviet government did not allow its citizens to emigrate freely. Beginning in 1971, however, a small number of Jews started to leave. They had the strong support of Jews in the United States, who helped to publicize the Soviet Union's discrimination against Jews. Congress passed the Jackson-Vanik Amendment, which forbade most-favored nation trading status for any country that restricted or taxed immigration. The legislation was aimed against the Soviet Union.

In the late 1980s the Soviets relaxed their emigration policy. Jewish emigration to the United States grew. The Hebrew Immigrant Aid Society, which had been helping Jewish immigrants

A Russian Jewish immigrant greets her mother who followed her to the United States. They started a new life in Texas.

On the Mariel Boatlift

Hamlet Arias came to the United States during the Mariel Boatlift from Cuba. He was only eight years old at the time and came with his grandmother. He remembered the journey:

"It was night. All that I remember, because I was so small, was my grandmother grabbing me by the arm, grabbing some of my clothes, putting them in a bag with some papers, and running out the door. We tried to take my older sister, but she had two kids and couldn't come.

"We were the last people to get on this boat. . . . It was just a fishing boat, built to hold about fifty people, but not for traveling across the ocean. There were many more people on this boat on that trip. Holding on to the sails, on top of the roof of the cabin, holding on to the sides of the boat.

"There were other people on lanchitas, which are little boats that are not meant to go too far ashore. . . . But the soldiers on other boats shot them down. I remember hearing a lot of gunfire, a lot of chasing, boats sinking. I saw about six or seven boats sink. I saw a person eaten by a shark. . . .

"In the daytime my grandmother stood over me the whole time so that I wouldn't get sunburned. I was seasick. All we had to eat were crackers and water. At night, it was pitch-black. All I could see was the moon and its reflection. I remember that somebody threw a wrapper from a cracker into the sea, and somebody jumped overboard and got it. By the second night, we arrived at Miami."

since before World War I, assisted these newcomers to find housing and jobs. The Soviet Jews formed a community in Brighton Beach, Brooklyn, with Soviet-style restaurants and pastry shops along Brighton Beach Avenue. After the breakup of the Soviet Union in 1991, immigrants poured in.

CENTRAL AMERICANS

In 1980 Congress passed the Refugee Act, which tried to set a comprehensive policy for the admission and resettlement of refugees. The Act adopted the United Nations definition of a refugee as a person having a well-founded fear of persecution in their homeland. Refugees could become permanent residents, persons eligible for citizenship, after one year in the country. A 50,000-person ceiling was established. The president needed to consult Congress before admitting additional refugees.

Despite the good intentions of the Act, Central American groups were treated unequally when they were seeking asylum. In the 1980s civil wars, death squads, and economic misery brought immigrants north from El Salvador, Guatemala, and Nicaragua in ever-larger numbers. The United States often welcomed Nicaraguan asylees, who were fleeing a government that Washington opposed. Guatemalan and Salvadoran asylees, whose governments were dictatorships that the United States approved of, were often intercepted and interned before being denied refugee status.

The journey was dangerous and this Cuban immigrant kissed the ground on his arrival.

CUBANS AND HAITIANS

Two Caribbean groups — Cubans and Haitians — were also treated differently. Cubans, because of their hostile relationship to an American foe, Fidel Castro, received favorable treatment when they arrived in the United States.

Congress in 1966 passed the Cuban Adjustment Act, which enabled Cubans who came after January 1, 1959, to acquire permanent status, the first step to citizenship. The elderly and infirm benefited from federally funded Cuban refugee programs. By 1980 Cubans living in the Miami Little Havana were second in population only to Havana itself. Moreover, the wealth of the Miami Cubans was greater than all the people in Cuba itself.

Haitians received a very different welcome. Haiti was as repressive a country as Cuba but did not have the "advantage" of a ruler who was an enemy of the United States. The different treatment of Haitians and Cubans was clearest during the Mariel Boatlift. In 1980 Castro allowed Cubans to leave the island from the port of Mariel. About 125,000 of these "Marielitos" left, many of them on boats that had been sent from southern Florida by Cuban Americans. At the same time Haitian peasants and urban poor took homemade boats to flee their homeland to come to the United States. Most of the Cuban Marielitos were allowed to stay, but the Haitians were denied asylum.

In 1994 American policy changed when President Bill Clinton ordered that any Cubans who were intercepted at sea would not automatically be given refugee status.

ILLEGAL IMMIGRATION

This demonstration in Chicago protests the treatment of immigrants, both legal and illegal.

Illegal immigration increased greatly from the 1970s on. Estimates of the numbers of illegal immigrants vary widely. Most experts believe at least 300,000 arrive each year.

MEXICAN ILLEGALS

Illegals come from all countries, but the most common are those who cross the border from Mexico. The 2,000-mile border is practically impossible to patrol, even though border-patrol agents use helicopters, motion sensors, and the latest in high-tech detection gadgets. In the early 1990s the federal government started constructing a fence along the 2000-mile border with Mexico. Made of corrugated steel, it is ten feet high with spikes along the top. By 1998 only sixty miles were completed.

On the Mexican side of the border, people known as "coyotes" help the illegal immigrants get across. They charge a high fee for the service and often cheat the would-be immigrants. In some cases, people are packed into trucks and driven through the desert. Some have died trying to enter the land of opportunity.

The journey to El Norte can start in small villages in Central America as well. Buses take people up the western coast of Mexico to Tijuana, directly across the border from San Diego, California. From there, they are on their own or must find a helpful "coyote." Asians and Europeans sometimes choose to enter through Mexico as well. They know that the U.S. Border Patrol at San Diego is less likely to closely examine anyone who does not look Latino.

SMUGGLING CHINESE

Chinese illegals are also numerous. Since Chinese farmers in the mid-1990s made around two hundred dollars a year, and factory workers only about twice that, even the lowest wages in the United States were considered very appealing.

Smuggling Chinese immigrants into this country is an organized business. Gangs are estimated to transport 50,000 to 80,000 illegals each year. The journey starts in China when a person wishing to go to the United States gets in touch with a guide called a "snakehead." The snakehead arranges for false passports and transportation. Since his fees are high, the potential immigrant is often helped by family and friends, who expect that he will send back the money with interest.

From China, there are many routes to the United States. Illegals are at the mercy of those who transport them along the way.

Even with the fence on the Mexican border, illegals still manage to get across.

Working "Off the Books"

An illegal immigrant from North Africa told an interviewer how he was able to find work in New York City without a green card that would legally enable him to find a job:

Q. You didn't have a work visa. So what kind of job did you find?

A. I had to find a job where people would pay me in cash. I had a lot of jobs. I worked in a deli, construction, busboy in a restaurant. They didn't ask for work papers. They just paid me in cash. They didn't even ask for my name.

Q. Were you cheated by any of these people you worked for?

A. Yes. Once. This was when I was really broke and needed a job, so I went to this man who owned a shish kebob restaurant, and he told me he needed a delivery boy. He said he'd pay me three dollars an hour, and I could also keep the tips from people I delivered to. So I worked the first day, and I was the dishwasher, cleaning the floors, and in the end I made only three deliveries. That brought me three dollars in tips. I had worked fourteen hours, so he owed me forty-two dollars. I had worked all day and I wasn't really doing deliveries as I'd been promised, but I said to myself, 'I need the money, so I won't say anything. Then I'll see what I'm going to do later.' Well, at the end of the day, the owner told me that this was just my training. He didn't pay me anything.

Q. So you didn't go back?

A. I didn't go back.

Many immigrants became citizens in the 1990s. In mass ceremonies, the new Americans pledged allegiance to their adopted country.

Some have even been packed into containers aboard ships. The journey may lead through Canada or Mexico, where immigrants are packed three to four in the trunk of a car. The ticket can cost from twenty-five thousand dollars to fifty thousand dollars, and an illegal who owes that amount of money may be kept in virtual slavery to pay off the debt.

One reason it is hard to catch illegal aliens is that their routes keep changing. One Coast Guard official was quoted in 1994: "It's like if you squeeze a balloon, it just pops out around your hand. If we tighten up, they're gonna look where we have a weak link."

Frustrated with the rising number of illegals, Congress passed another immigration law in 1986. It provided amnesty, or forgiveness, to all illegal aliens who had lived in the United States since before January 1, 1982.

The law also set penalties for employers who knowingly hired illegal aliens in the future. For the first time, employers were responsible for checking the legality of their workers. However, large agricultural employers were protected, taking some of the teeth out of the new law.

If caught, illegal aliens have the right under United States law to fight deportation. If they can launch a strong case on humanitarian grounds, they sometimes can get refugee status. To do so, immigrants must show they will be persecuted in their home countries for religious beliefs, racial background, or membership in a political organization. If Chinese, they can try to make their case against the country's population-control policies. In the past, the Immigration and Naturalization Service often released illegal immigrants, warning them to return for a hearing on a specific date. Many did not show up. Today, most are kept in special holding facilities that are overcrowded.

These Haitian immigrants arrived in Florida in 1980. It takes at least three days for such a journey.

Louis Jobel from El Salvador is a master bootmaker who learned his craft from his father.

Today's immigrants arrive with the widest possible range of job skills. Some have advanced degrees in science and medicine. Others come with nothing but ambition and a limitless capacity for hard work. Juan Carrera, who came from the Dominican Republic, is now a successful manager in a food store. He remembered: "Things were difficult for me, but I attacked. I attacked by working hard. I like to work. And I got good things out of life."

LOW-PAYING JOBS

Just as in the past, unskilled immigrants today work in the low-paid manufacturing sector. This means jobs in sweatshops making clothing, shoes, or other basic items. In fact, the large number of available immigrants — including illegals, who would work for low wages — actually stimulated the growth of such industries as apparel and leather goods. The poor wages and working conditions were unattractive to most Americans, but immigrants were eager to take them.

Illegal immigrants find jobs as gardeners, cooks, and nannies, where they can be paid "off the books," without proper identification. Employers do not have the expense of paying for their health insurance or Social Security benefits. These "underground economy" jobs increased in the 1980s.

Even so, many refugees depend on public assistance programs to survive. Cambodians, Hmong, and Laotians, for example, had a particularly hard time adjusting. The leader of the Cambodian community in Long Beach, California, Sovann Tith, explained: "Most Cambodians here are farmers with only four years of education; now they live in urban America."

Sukhwant Gill, a Sikh from India, works on his family farm in California, which specializes in seedless grapes.

Finding a Job

Elan Liberman, an immigrant from Israel, describes the jobs he found after arriving in New York City around 1969:

"My uncle got me a Social Security card. It was easier to get in those days if you didn't have a green card. And a day later I had a job on North Moore Street. Some warehouse. He had arranged it with someone. What do you do in a warehouse? The trucks come, you load and unload them, and I was driving a forklift.

"I was paid in cash, working off the books because I didn't have a green card. Then there was a big snowfall, and they had to let some people go. I was laid off, but they said I could come back later when things got busier.

"Meanwhile, I enrolled in an advertising school for a few months. I got a job with a small ad agency and worked in the art department for a while. One thing I learned was that you had to read a newspaper every day to improve your English. At that time, there were many stories about Israel in the newspaper, so I knew sort of what they were writing about. Reading the articles was easier for me, even if I missed a few words. I would underline the words I didn't know and look them up in a dictionary in the evening. That way, I learned more about the United States, too.

"The ad agency laid me off because they lost an account, and I found another job selling Electrolux vacuum cleaners door-to-door. In the first few weeks, I made as much as four hundred dollars a week. I was pretty good getting into buildings, through the service entrance. It was a good vacuum cleaner, and once I got in and could demonstrate it, they would buy it.

"Mostly I met people's maids, and they were easier to deal with. I convinced the maids that the vacuum cleaner would be easier to use, and she would go in to see the woman who lived there, and come back with a check. I was pretty good. So I saved up enough money to go to college."

PROFESSIONALS AND HIGH-TECH WORKERS

Middle-class and elite professionals are also represented among today's immigrants. The medical profession relies heavily on immigrants to fully staff urban hospitals and doctors' offices in rural areas. Asians are found at all levels of the medical field. Chinese, Koreans, Filipinos, Pakistanis, and Indians are hospital workers in most big cities. One out of every six doctors in Ohio is from South Asia. Immigrants are also numerous among pharmacists and dentists.

Indians and other Asians are also important to today's high-tech industries. The federal government has

Immigrants of today often come with high-tech and business skills, like this manager from Africa.

A Filipino Doctor's Story

Armando Tabotabo was born in the Philippines, and trained as a doctor.
He came to the United States in 1966.

"I had decided to leave the Philippines around 1957. The living conditions are not as good as they are here. People don't have so much money there, and they don't have many job opportunities. Also there is no dignity of labor. By this I mean that if you are a student and you take a job as a department-store salesman, people will tend to look down on you, especially if you are from a middle-class family. You're not supposed to work if you are rich. Work is supposed to be shameful.

"I left the Philippines in 1966. I thought I could make a better life for myself here. I thought I would have a better chance as a doctor. My aunt and uncle in Honolulu and a lot of friends and classmates who had come here told me about this country. I also read about it a lot, because it was

my dream to come here, especially New York City.

"I came by plane. My aunt and uncle met me at Honolulu International Airport. When I came through immigration they checked my X rays again. If I had shown evidence of tuberculosis they wouldn't have let me in. They don't take the readings of the Filipino doctors — not because they feel that the doctors don't know how to read X rays, but because they feel that the doctor may be your friend and may have read the X rays as normal so you can get in.

"My destination was Pittsburgh. I worked for one year at a hospital there, doing my internship all over again. Everyone was very nice. I've been to several places in the United States, and I think Pittsburgh people are the friendliest."

created a special visa, called H1-B. This is given to immigrants, above the quota limits, at the request of high-tech companies. Such companies as Microsoft and Intel say they need foreign high-tech specialists to work "temporarily" in the United States for up to six years.

Over half of these special visa holders are Indian and Chinese. The rest are divided among British, Filipinos, Canadians, Japanese, Germans, Pakistanis, and French. Russians and immigrants from the republics of the former Soviet Union, as well as Israelis, are also employed by high-tech companies. These highly skilled professionals, however, often find they are paid less than other employees. In some ways they are like the indentured laborers of old, because they are here to work for specific companies. If they quit their jobs, their visas would be terminated. Others end up in so-called body shops — high-tech sweatshops — pounding out computer code.

Other workers from Asia, Mexico, and other countries make computer chips. The work is repetitious and boring but requires constant concentration and perfect eye-hand coordination to manipulate the tiny, intricate circuitry. Some production processes involve toxic chemicals and the rate of occupational illnesses is three times the average for all industries.

STARTING NEW BUSINESSES

Many of the new immigrants have become successful entrepreneurs. Some have founded high-tech firms; others are among the management of these new companies. These entrepreneurs represent the most successful of today's immigrants, and their Mercedeses and Jaguars announce their wealth.

Chicago is home to many Mexican immigrants. This man is the proud owner of a butcher shop there.

Nearly three fourths of all Korean immigrants work for themselves or for other Koreans. Usually, the whole family works in the business. Korean-American credit unions lend money to make it possible for their members to start businesses. The Koreans became dominant in the fruit-and-vegetable business in New York City during the 1980s. Koreans also own gas stations, nail parlors, and beauty parlors, as well as small garment factories, fish stores, and dry cleaners.

South Asians, especially Indians, have also been successful as business owners. They started with ethnic enterprises, such as clothing shops that catered to Indian woman or grocery stores that stocked Indian foods. Then they branched out. Today, the motel business in the United States is dominated by Indian Americans.

Cuban Americans are often cited as pioneering the modern immigrant success story. Antonio Jorge, a Cuban immigrant, described the pattern: "Our sense of identity was related to our economic success. If we had not kept together . . . if we had blended with the surrounding community; if we had not built an enclave of our own; if we had not created a market for ourselves, then we would not have been economically successful."

The *quinceañera* party of this fifteen-year-old in Chicago shows the blend of cultures. Behind the honored girl are images of the Beatles, a Mexican zoot-suiter (a popular style of the 1940s), and Marilyn Monroe.

CHAPTER TWELVE

A NEW AMERICA

M. Elaine Mar came to the United States from Hong Kong when she was five years old. In her memoir *Paper Daughter*, she described how her relatives practiced the Chinese custom of honoring their ancestors.

"Aunt Becky displayed Buddhist figurines on the TV set. Mother talked about Taoist principles of moderation, and Father liked to quote Confucius and Mao in equal measure. But luck was our true religion. In the name of luck, we ate chicken, wore red, and lit joss sticks on holy days. In the name of luck, we prayed to our ancestors. As far as my family was concerned, Memorial Day was the most important and most solemn holiday of the year. On this day we woke up early to pay respects to our dead ancestors, a tradition the Chinese call 'walking the mountain.'

"We filled the trunk of Becky's Chevrolet with potted flowers and drove to Fairmount Cemetery. . . . Aunt Becky drove, and as the road wound more deeply into the cemetery, gravestones flattened into discreet plaques. . . .

"When we finally found the marker, Aunt Becky knelt to pull the grass that had grown up on its borders. She left flowers on the ground and stood. Uncle Andy and Father stepped forward and kowtowed. At his mother's urging, San [her cousin] followed their example. He clasped his hands together and bowed three times, saying, 'Let me be a good boy and honor my family in the coming year.'

"'Me too?' I asked Mother excitedly, although I couldn't decipher who exactly the ancestor was.

"She laughed. 'No, not you. You're a girl.' . . .

"That's not fair, I thought. . . . I decided to kowtow in my head, where my family couldn't see. After all, they were my dead ancestors, too."

The new immigrants of today are building their own communities. They are preserving their own traditions as they blend into the new America, which is partly their creation as well.

Scouting has been a popular Americanizer since the early 1900s. These Filipino Boy Scouts are part of a troop in New York City.

Like immigrants of the past, today's newcomers often want to live among their own people. The comfort of a familiar language, food, and lifestyle is strong. Koreatown in Los Angeles is an example. The neighborhood around Olympic Boulevard is the heart of a Korean community of 150,000 people. The churches, travel agencies, night clubs, and restaurants make the immigrants feel right at home. Here Korean is spoken and understood. "One does not feel that one lives in America," remarked a Korean immigrant, "when one lives on Olympic Boulevard."

Mexican immigrant Danny Romero described the importance of the barrio: "The barrio is a place where you can speak Spanish freely, if you choose to do so, and both be understood and accepted. In the barrio you can be Chicano, or Mexican, or Puerto Rican [and more recently, Salvadoran, Guatemalan, or Dominican]. The barrio is a place where, for the most part, you are safe from your person being wrongly judged just because of your ethnicity, your accent, or your taste in clothes, food, or music."

TWO NEW YORK COMMUNITIES

Two communities in New York City are typical of neighborhoods where the new immigrants have chosen to live. Manhattan's Chinatown has been home to Chinese immigrants since the 1800s. Today more than 150,000 people live there in a few small blocks. The majority of them were born outside the United States. Older residents — second- and third-generation Chinese Americans — have moved to the suburbs. They return to Chinatown only on weekends to shop. The population of today's Chinatown comes from Taiwan, Singapore, Vietnam, Malaysia, and many parts of China. Chinatown newcomers arrive with families, so the bachelor society is disappearing.

Those Chinese who arrive with valuable skills and money usually find good jobs and become part of American society very quickly. For poorer Chinese immigrants, Chinatown is both workplace and home —

a place where an immigrant does not have to speak English. Many illegals are here, too, working in the sweatshops on upper stories of small buildings. They blend in with the population, making them feel secure.

Several miles east, in the borough of Brooklyn, is the Soviet-Jewish neighborhood called "Little Odessa," after a city on the Black Sea that many of its residents came from. When the Soviet immigrants first arrived in the 1970s, Brighton Beach was a decaying neighborhood. It got a jolt of energy from the newcomers who settled there. Word spread that there were large apartments by the sea. One Odessan noted, "The first time I saw the boardwalk and the beach, I decided I wanted to live here. It reminds me a little of home." Brighton Beach became the largest Soviet émigré colony in the world. Signs in the Cyrillic (Russian) alphabet replaced Yiddish and English signs on the stores. Russian-style nightclubs sprang up.

OTHER NEW COMMUNITIES

Other new immigrant communities include Huntington Park, California, now the most "Mexican" city in the United States. Locally known as HP, it is located just east of Los Angeles. Almost 60 percent of the 50,000 residents were born in Mexico. Others came from Guatemala, El Salvador, Cuba, and Puerto Rico. The only majority-Asian city in the United States is Monterey Park, also in California, with a population that is more than 56 percent Asian.

This immigrant family lives in New Bedford, Massachusetts, the home of many other Portuguese Americans.

The Big Fifteenth Birthday

Blanca Ortiz came to California from Mexico and now owns a clothing store. She describes the *quinceanera*, the gala celebration of a girl's fifteenth birthday.

"The quinceanera is celebrated so she can pass from being a girl to being a lady. For many girls this is a very serious occasion, something that has to be done right, like your first communion. To other girls it just means have a big party, but all of them go to a special Mass before they party.

"The boy who is dearest to the quinceanera is the one she chooses as her partner for the day, and her close friends make up the other seven couples. She always has fifteen attendants. We call the girls damas.

"All the quinceaneras — when they first come in here to choose the dress, the hat, the gloves, shoes, rosary — are bright-eyed and excited about the fuss that is made over them. To choose the right kind of dress is not always easy. The girl has to consider not only her own parents' pocketbook but also that of her friends' parents, since every girl pays for her own dress. When everything is settled and down payment has been made, she brings all the girls in to be measured and they make their down payment. For the next three or four months she and her damas make payments every two weeks. After the final fitting they pick up their dress, and we expect full payment at that time. For some girls this is a big expense. Their parents might not earn so much. But every Mexican girl wants to celebrate her quinceanera."

Indians are scattered throughout the United States but have centers in Queens, New York, and in Chicago around Devon Street, which is also known as "Patel Nagar." Stores selling Indian spices and saris are sprinkled through the neighborhood along with restaurants and travel agencies. Women often wear the *salwar-kameez,* or tunic and pants, as well as an occasional sari.

These new immigrants are not only going to the cities as they tended to in the past. Today many settle in the suburbs and even rural areas as well.

CHILDREN AND THE FAMILY

One of the strongest desires of many immigrants is to see their children advance. Parents see their own work as building for their children's future. Dagnachew Mengesha, an immigrant from Ethiopia, explained, "I feel like I'll always be able to find a job and take care of my family. This is the most important thing for a man."

But the immigrant experience puts a great deal of pressure on the family. Rarely will all the generations of a family come to the United States at the same time. The separation causes pain. Not all family members may adapt equally well to the new country. Parents always have the pull of their past lives. Children are more likely to learn how to get along in a new culture.

Because children usually pick up English faster than their parents, they often play a leading role in helping the family to adjust to their new circumstances. This is a reversal of the traditional role of parent and child and often causes conflict. "In Korea we are considered to be children until we are eighteen years old or more. We are at all times told what to do; we learn to follow instructions," Sung Han Kim, a Korean immigrant, explains.

Immigrant children often feel trapped between their parents' demands to keep traditional standards and their own desire to become as American as possible. Dating of adolescent girls is often a source of conflict. An Armenian immigrant girl said, "Armenian parents are very strict. Often they stop their kids from going to dances. . . . My parents are not that free, either, but they trust me and let me go. . . . But we cannot have boyfriends. Once we have a friend, we have to get engaged to get married."

The new culture often has different roles for the men and women and family members than was found in the home country. A Dominican woman noted that the working experience changed her role in the family and her relationship with her husband: "We are both the heads. If both husband and wife are earning salaries then they should equally rule the household. In the Dominican Republic it is always the husband who gives the orders in the household. But here when the two are working, the woman feels herself equal to the man in the ruling of the home."

The Balinos—father and sons, immigrants from Argentina—pose proudly in their store in Elmhurst, Queens, in New York City.

SCHOOL

These two school girls, from Yemen and Egypt, stand near the mosque in Dearborn, Michigan, home to many Arab immigrants.

Most immigrants place great faith in the value of education. The desire for a college education attracts many talented people to the United States. For in some societies, acceptance to a university is very difficult to get unless one's family is rich or powerful. Ralph Onugu, who was raised in Nigeria, feared that he could never get a slot in the university. "I didn't want to spend my life cleaning the rich man's office," he said, "which would have been my only choice in Nigeria if I didn't have an education. I wanted to be sitting in that desk myself."

Immigrants make up a growing proportion of the students in the public schools of American big cities. As immigrants did in the early years of the 1900s, they often bring special needs to class. Those who have fled their countries as refugees, for example, have no records or transcript of earlier schooling. Others, due to war and revolution, have had little or no education. Some refugees from Cambodia are in this category.

Narong Phon, a Cambodian immigrant who works in San Diego helping fellow immigrants noted "The younger people who come to the United States had no schooling in Cambodia and no schooling during the five years they stayed in the Thailand refugee camp. They never learned to read or write their own language. . . . How can you teach them English when they don't know a verb from a noun? All they know is how to plant rice with their hands."

LEARNING ENGLISH

Many immigrants speak little English and need special instruction to bring their English skills up to the level of their classmates. The U.S. Supreme Court ruled in 1974 that non-English-speaking children had a right to equal opportunity with English-speaking children. In the case

Lau v. *Nichols* a majority of the Court said that school districts must provide children who speak little or no English with special language programs to give them that equal opportunity. This sometimes challenges schools where immigrants form a substantial number. In some schools in New York City, the students speak more than thirty languages.

Using flash cards, two Hmong first graders are learning English in their school in Fresno, California.

Alfida del Rosario came from the Dominican Republic to Washington Heights, a Manhattan neighborhood, when she was ten. "School was exciting," she remembered, "because I liked everything about learning. Meeting new people. But it was also scary, because if you don't know the language they do pick on you. They do that a lot. I never liked English. I don't know if it was because of the criticism of the students or because I didn't face that in my country. Kids are mean at that age. When I started taking classes, I did take ESL — English as a Second Language — until high school. The rest of my classes were taught in Spanish. I thought my teachers were very nice. I learned a lot from them."

Learning English is not the only goal for immigrants. Many want their children to be able to read and write in the language of their homeland. In order to guarantee this, many immigrant groups have established their own schools to teach the language and history and culture of their homeland. Haroutian Yeretzian, an Armenian immigrant who came from Lebanon noted, "My son goes to an Armenian school. When he comes home from school he immediately turns on the TV. We fight with him every day; learn your Armenian lessons!"

The children in this Florida school are refugees whose families fled from the fighting in the former Yugoslavia.

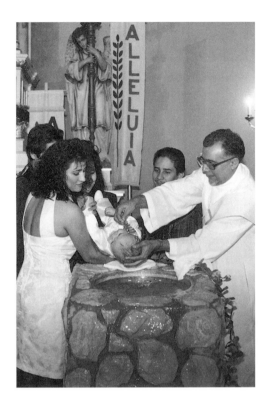

At this baptism, the godparents stand with the parents and assume some responsibility for the child, as is the Mexican custom.

Today's new immigrants have revitalized the three traditional religions of America — Protestantism, Roman Catholicism, and Judaism. Protestantism has been particularly enriched by immigrants from the Caribbean, Korea, and some African countries. The church is the center of the Korean community. It is a place to meet people, learn about business opportunities, and celebrate the Korean heritage. Pastors and officers in the church are important leaders of Korean-American communities.

The Roman Catholic church has long been a support for immigrants. It has been strengthened by the large number of recent immigrants who have come from Latin America. The face of the Catholic Church is changing, with a growing number of services in Spanish or Portuguese. Many Catholics have also come from Vietnam and Europe.

Judaism has been rejuvenated by the arrival of Israelis and Jews from the former Soviet Union. When they first arrived, many Soviet Jews did not know how to practice some parts of their religion, because the Soviet Union was an atheist country that discouraged all forms of religious worship. Indeed, for many immigrants it was the ability to renew their ties with Judaism that made their immigration most meaningful.

NEW RELIGIONS

The new immigrants have added to the variety of American religions. Islam is one of the fastest growing religions in the United States today. The earlier Arab immigration was mainly Christian. Today, most are Muslims, as are such other Middle Eastern immigrants as Iranians, Afghans, and Turks. Muslims also come from some African countries, and Pakistan, India, and Bangladesh. Abdel Selam Saleh, from Jordan, said, "We feel free here in the United States to practice our religion. The people who come here [the Islamic Center of Southern California] to worship are from many different countries and continents."

Buddhism is another growing religion in the United States. It is

Keeping the Faith

Sarbit Singh from India is a member of the Sikh religion. He described how he had to sacrifice to keep his religion in the United States:

"Being a Sikh, I have a long beard, I have a turban. I wanted to join the Army or the California Highway Patrol, but I was told that at certain times I would be required to wear a mask that would not fit over my beard. I would therefore have to shave in order to join. I told them that technology is very advanced, we don't let our beard flow when we work, we fix it so the hair is tied to the skin. They can design a mask which can be pulled over the beard and over the turban. But they say they can't do that for one or two persons. If you want to join, they say, you have to shave. Well, I was not able to join them. The hair is a living part of my body and I was taught to respect it because I was made in the image of God. My masters fought for their religion; some sacrificed their life. My religion is valuable to me. I can give up my life, but I can't cut my hair."

practiced by some Vietnamese, Chinese, Japanese, and Southeast Asian immigrants. Buddhist temples are found today in many states. The temple or *vihara* becomes the center of social activities and attracts worshipers from all over the surrounding area. Paisarn Burana, an immigrant from Thailand, attends a Buddhist temple in Los Angeles. He said, "People come here from as far as Santa Barbara, Orange County, and San Diego, since this is the only big Thai temple in southern California."

Hinduism is the faith of the majority of Indian immigrants. Hindus have important home rituals that need *puja* rooms, or shrines. Some Indian immigrants convert kitchen cupboards or closets into worship centers. They also worship in Hindu temples that are often placed near water and mountains, reminders of India. The first large Hindu temple in Los Angeles was built in the Malibu hills near the ocean and modeled on a temple in southern India.

Like other religions, Hinduism is being influenced by life in the United States. The Hindu Vedic University of America in San Diego is pioneering the teaching of Hinduism on computers.

Buddhism is one of the fastest growing religions in the United States today. Thai monks celebrate the New Year in a New York temple.

The number of immigrants seeking citizenship has grown tremendously. Here, a stadium full of new Americans takes the oath of citizenship.

While running for president in 1980, Ronald Reagan expressed an optimistic view of immigration: "Can we doubt that only a divine Providence placed this land of freedom here as a refuge for all those people in the world who yearn to breathe free?" he asked. To some the answer was yes. Many Americans felt threatened by the large number of immigrants.

SPEAKING ENGLISH

Some Americans fear that English will no longer be the primary language of the United States. In 1990 more than 32 million Americans spoke English as a second language. More than half of these spoke Spanish as their primary tongue. In many large cities, there are not only Spanish-language newspapers but also TV and radio stations that broadcast in Spanish. In some areas such as southern Florida, official notices and election ballots are in both English and Spanish.

The question is, does it harm the country if more than one language is in common use? A second, related question is, should schools teach immigrant students in the language they already know, or should every child be taught in English? A look at history shows that this is not the first time these questions have been raised. German was once as common a language in some communities as Spanish is now. Experience has shown that immigrant children pick up the use of English quickly, as long as they find it useful.

And most immigrants do learn English. Sam Aronov arrived in New York with his wife and son from the Soviet Union in 1972. He recalled: "We found an apartment, but we needed to furnish it. We picked up some furniture from the street. I found a TV that worked, because I knew that from the TV I could learn English. When I listened to the TV, I started to understand what people said to me."

Preserving the Heritage

Alfida del Rosaro came to the United States from the Dominican Republic when she was ten years old. She is proud of her culture and described how she celebrated her heritage:

"We celebrated American holidays as well as Dominican holidays. Christmas is a little different. On January 6 in the Dominican Republic, they celebrate Los Tres Reyes Magos — the Three Kings. That is the day that parents hide gifts under our bed, while we are sleeping, so that when we wake up we would look for them and open the gifts. Only the children receive gifts. Christmas Day is basically for eating lots of food and dancing. And on January 6 we get the gifts. On February 27, Independence Day is celebrated. We just had a special meal at home.

"In the Dominican Republic they celebrate Independence Day — I don't know how to translate it, but they call it diablo cajuelos. It's basically like Halloween. People dress up and wear lots of colors, with masks like the faces of animals, and they use things that make noises. There is some kind of parade. Something else called San André when people take handfuls of flour and throw it at you. I didn't like that or the hitting of a bunch of balloons wrapped up in a stick.

"I like all Dominican food including their exotic fruits. We customarily eat what we call 'the flag'— rice, beans, and some sort of meat. Also fried plantains and salad are favorites."

AMERICANIZATION TODAY

Every immigrant was changed personally in his or her journey to this country. A Soviet Jewish immigrant commented: "To immigrate is not just to cross an ocean. It is to enter a whole new world." Facing the different life in a new country, each person makes his or her own blend of old and new. Some keep more of their customs and fashions than others. Clothes are an immediate concern because everyone notices what one wears. A century ago, many immigrants made a trip to the clothing store, one of their first stops in America.

Today, immigrants want to keep part of their clothing tradition. The Hmong from Laos have a tradition of wearing clothes with

At this Haitian Festival parade in Florida, a young girl waves to the crowd from an elaborate float.

Outside American, Inside Portuguese

Jorge Manuel Pereira immigrated in 1980 from Portugal with his family. They lived in a Portuguese community in New Bedford, Massachusetts. He described how the move had affected his family:

"In Portugal, my father was the decision-maker but here, decision-making is a family process. We all talk about how things are going to be done. When my father had to buy a car, we all decided. It would be a family car and everybody was going to help pay for it. Moving from one house to another was another joint decision. . . .

"We were American on the outside, but as soon as you stepped into our house, you were in Portugal. We spoke only Portuguese. Everything in the house breathed Portuguese, the food, the smells, the knickknacks, the books. We watched Portuguese TV, listened to Portuguese radio. The house was like a little Portugal. . . .

"Over the years, we have become more

Americanized. We watch American television. . . . We've become like every American family, ordering things from catalogues, having a check book, using credit cards. So I'm very Portuguese and at the same time I'm very American. . . .

"My brother is an American, he's not Portuguese anymore. He came when he was 12 and he's become part of this culture. . . . So much depends on the age you come. My brother has almost no accent compared to me and my sisters. He doesn't like Portuguese music, he likes rock and roll. He doesn't read books in Portuguese as my sisters and I do. Every time there is some Portuguese event, we have to drag him."

Traditional dances from India are brought to the United States and enjoyed by the immigrant community in Texas.

very elaborate embroidery. It can take a year to make a traditional outfit. Vue Chou, a Hmong immigrant, still loves to sew and embroider but she only wears traditional clothes for special occasions. "American clothes are easy to get, easy to wear, easy to make," she says. "Now we use our traditional clothes only on New Year's or for a big party."

Many Indian women have continued to wear the wraparound sari, traditional in their homeland. Shreelekha Mohanty started out keeping much of the Indian traditional style. Over time, she made some changes for convenience: "When I came from India, I was still wearing the traditional sari, and people used to stare at me. A little kid thought my forehead was bleeding because I had the red dot, the *bindi;* married women are supposed to wear the *bindi.* One time when I was vacuuming, the end of the sari got into the vacuum cleaner and it almost got sucked in. That's when I said, 'Okay, it's time for me to change!'"

Zarina Sidi took the opposite path. She came to this country from Kenya, took college courses, and did some home-nursing. She noted: "Growing up in Kenya I always thought of skyscrapers and cowboys in America, whereas there are neither in the town where I'm working. I enjoy wearing my traditional Kanga while I'm here. It's like a little piece of home I can take with me."

A Panamanian dancer whirls around the floor at the Texas Folklife Festival, which celebrates the multicultural heritage of Texas.

THE AMERICAN DREAM TODAY

Immigrants have changed the United States as well. The transformation is now and always has been a two-way process. Every immigrant brought, and brings, new energies and possibilities to our country. In exchange for the effort, America offers freedom and a chance to do better for oneself or one's children.

Immigrants themselves express this feeling best in their own words. Andres Arias from El Salvador: "This is a beautiful country. It gives you many opportunities."

Phu Nguyen from Vietnam: "I came here with nothing, but I feel lucky because I had a dream and the opportunity to make that dream come true. . . . I came here to build, to do what I did not have a chance to do in Vietnam."

Eskiender "Alex" Mehari from Ethiopia: "You can be yourself here in a way that's impossible in many other countries. . . . You can even create your own job and your own religion if you want. . . . The pioneer spirit still exists very strongly in this country. I'm an American now. I feel like a modern-day pioneer."

The dreams that the immigrants brought with them became the heart of the American dream itself.

FURTHER READING

Berrol, Selma Cantor, *Growing Up American: Immigrant Children in America Then and Now,* Twayne Publishers, New York, 1995.

Daniels, Roger, *Coming to America: A History of Immigration and Ethnicity in American Life,* Harper Perennial, New York, 1991.

Dublin, Thomas, ed., *Immigrant Voices: New Lives in America 1773-1986,* University of Illinois Press, Urbana and Chicago, 1993.

Editors of Time-Life Books, *Immigrants: the New Americans,* Time-Life Books, Alexandria, VA, 1999.

Gonzalez, Juan, *Harvest of Empire: A History of Latinos in America,* Viking, New York, 2000.

Grossman, Sari and Schur, Joan Brodsky, eds., *In a New Land: An Anthology of Immigrant Literature,* National Textbook Co., Lincolnwood, IL, 1996.

Hoobler, Dorothy, and Hoobler, Thomas, *The American Family Albums,* Oxford University Press, New York, 1994-1997.

The African American Family Album

The Chinese American Family Album

The Cuban American Family Album

The German American Family Album

The Irish American Family Album

The Italian American Family Album

The Japanese American Family Album

The Jewish American Family Album

The Mexican American Family Album

The Scandinavian American Family Album

Stade, Bruce M. and Sutherland, Joan F., with Aldo Salerno, *From the Old Country: An Oral History of European Migration to America,* Twayne Publishers, New York, 1994.

Strom, Yale, *Quilted Landscape: Conversations with Young Immigrants,* Simon & Schuster Books for Young Readers, New York, 1996.

Ungar, Sanford J., *Fresh Blood: the New American Immigrants,* University of Illinois Press, Urbana and Chicago, 1998.

Yans-McLaughlin, Virginia, and Lightman, Marjorie, *Ellis Island and the Peopling of America,* The New Press, New York, 1997.

Zia, Helen, *Asian American Dreams: The Emergence of an American People,* Farrar, Straus and Giroux, New York, 2000.

Zucker, Norman L., and Zucker, Naomi Flink, *Desperate Crossing: Seeking Refuge in America,* M.E. Sharpe, Armonk, NY, 1996.

INDEX

CREDITS

ART CREDITS

American Antiquarian Society: 44 bottom; American Historical Society of Germans from Russia: 116; American Jewish Archives: 25; AP/Wide World Photos: 179, 184; George Ardealean Photo Group, The Balch Institute for Ethnic Studies: 126 bottom; Arizona Historical Society: 140; Atlantis Photo Group, The Balch Institute for Ethnic Studies: 113 top; Balch Broadside Collection, The Balch Institute for Ethnic Studies: 136; Bancroft Library: 76; Bishop Museum: 102; Bodziak Photo Group, The Balch Institute for Ethnic Studies: 125 bottom; Border Heritage Collection, El Paso Public Library, El Paso, TX: 141; Courtesy of the Bostonian Society, Old State House: 50, 77; Brown Brothers: 154; California Historical Society: FN-04470, 64; Calumet Regional Archives, Indiana University Northwest: 128; Chicago Historical Society: #ICHi-04077, 139; Courtesy of the Chippewa Valley Museum, Eau Claire, Wisconsin: 67, 162 (John Lindrud, *Eau Claire Leader-Telegram*); Colonial Williamsburg Foundation: 16, 24, 31; Courtesy of the Colorado Historical Society: #F-4259, 12; Corbis: 148, 168; Culver Pictures: 44 top; Cumberland County (PA) Historical Society: 18 (both); Danish Emigration Archive: 90 bottom; *Fresno Bee*: 115, 122, 170 (both), 181 top; German Information Office, New York City: 41; Hagley Museum and Library: 53 top; Hawaii State Archives: 125; Hedmarks Museet og Domkirkeodden: 53 bottom; Lewis W. Hine, George Eastman House: 105, 106 top; Lewis W. Hine Collection, Milstein Division of United States History, Local History and Genealogy, The New York Public Library, Astor, Lenox, and Tilden Foundations: 103, 118; Historical Association of Southern Florida: 165, 185; Historical Museum of Southern Florida: 155; The Historical Society of Pennsylvania: *Fourth of July Celebration in Centre Square,* John Lewis Krimmel, [Bc 882 K897], title page, 38 (detail); The Huntington Library, San Marino, California, Pierce 4376: 74; Idaho State Historical Society: 95; Illinois Labor History Society: 147 top; Immigrant City Archives: 60, 119, 121, 126 top, 134, 161; Immigration History Research Center, University of Minnesota (Alexander A. Granovsky Papers, Box 50): 131; Institute of Texan Cultures: 35, 37 (Courtesy José Cisneros), 70, 96 top; 96 bottom, 156, 163, 186, 187; Italian Community Center, Milwaukee: 100; Kansas Collection: 132; Kansas State Historical Society: 86; Courtesy of the Lane County Historical Museum: 92 top; Corky Lee: 176, 183; Library and Archives Division, Historical Society of Western Pennsylvania, Pittsburgh, PA: 127; Library of Congress: 22, 28 top, 34, 48, 83, 90 top, 98, 113, 114, 120, 144, 146, 147 bottom, 150; Collections of Maine Historical Society: 130 (#6345-47); Maine State Archives: 142 top; Manchester (NH) Historic Association: 58; Jacob Rader Marcus Center of the American Jewish Archives: 80; David Maung: 167; From the Milwaukee Public Library Collection: 66; Minnesota Historical Society: 87; Missouri Historical Society, St. Louis: 69 (Thomas M. Easterly); Alice Murata: 110; Musée de l'Homme, Paris: 28 bottom; Courtesy of the UBC Museum of Anthropology, Vancouver, Canada: 17; Museum of the City of New York: *Five Points, 1827,* From Valentine's Manual, Lithographers: McSpedon & Baker, c. 1850, Museum of the City of New York, Gift of Lou Sepersky & Leida Snow: 61; *Jewish Girl with American Flag*, Museum of the City of New York, Jacob Riis Collection (449): 6 bottom right; Nicolino Calyo, *The Oyster Stand,* Watercolor 10 1/4" x 14", c. 1840-1844, Museum of the City of New York, Gift of Mrs. Francis P. Garvan in memory of Francis P. Garvan, 55.6.16: 56 top; © Mystic Seaport, Mystic, CT: 59; Museum of History and Industry: 124; National Anthropological Archives, Smithsonian Institution: #77-2861, 8; National Archives: 13, 106 bottom, 109, 149, 153; National Archives, Pacific Sierra Region: 108 (both); Courtesy of the National Park Service, U.S. Department of the Interior: 27, 85, 101, 104, 107, 137, 142 bottom; Nebraska Historical Society: 73; Collection of the New-York Historical Society #44314, 26; #74985, 30; #63911, 42; #44326, 54 bottom; #41526, 81; New York State Library: 40, 47, 52, 54 top; North Dakota Institute for Regional Studies: 78; Oakland Museum of California, gift of anonymous donor: 75; Ohio Historical Society: 14 (all); Oregon Historical Society: 6 top (#118GO15), 152 (#OrHi 58758); Courtesy of the Oregon Jewish Museum: 72; Antonio Perez: 7 top, 166, 171, 173, 174, 182; Pollard Memorial Library, Lowell, MA: 56 bottom; Presbyterian Historical Society, Presbyterian Church (U.S.A) (Philadelphia): 32; Pueblo City-County Library District: 123; Millicent Rogers Museum: 36; Shades of L.A. Archives/Los Angeles Public Library: 157; Slater Mill Historical Society: 46; Southern Pacific Railroad: 84; Courtesy of the Southwest Museum, Los Angeles: #N22,651, 10; Spinner Publications, Inc.: 177; State Historical Society of North Dakota: 89 bottom; Staten Island Historical Society: 6 bottom left; Photo by Yale Strom from his book *Quilted Landscapes: Conversations with Immigrant Youth,* Simon and Schuster: 180; Arthur Szyk, Reproduced with permission of Alexandra Szyk Bracie in cooperation with Irvin Ungar and the Arthur Szyk Society, Burlingame, California: 20, 71 (both reproductions Courtesy The Kosciuszko Foundation); United Nations High Commissioner for Refugees (UNHCR): 158, 169; UNHCR/B. Press: 181 bottom; UNHCR/8268/1978/K. Gaugler: 162; Utah State Historical Society: 7 bottom; Vesterheim Norwegian American Museum: 89 top; The Western Reserve Historical Society, Cleveland, Ohio: 138; Wisconsin Historical Society: #Whi (K3) 30348, 15; #Whi (X3) 42083, 62 top; #Whi (V22) 1387 [Charles J. Van Schaick], 92 bottom.

TEXT SOURCES AND CREDITS

6, Polvi: Damrell, Joseph, ed., *Isaac Polvi: The Autobiography of a Finnish Immigrant* (St. Cloud, MN: North Star Press of St. Cloud, 1991), p. 127. • 9, "Ice . . .": • 15, DeVries: Rae, Noel, comp. & ed., *Witnessing America* (New York: Penguin, 1996), p. 254. • 16, Magalopensis: Rae, Noel, *op. cit.*, p. 20. • 16, Delaware Indians: *Ibid.*, pp. 55-56. • 17, Navajo boy: Nabokov, Peter, ed., *Native American Testimony* (New York, Penguin, 1991), p. 31. • 17, Iron Teeth: Josephy, Alvin M., Jr., *500 Nations* (New York: Knopf, 1994), p. 354. • 18, Bercier: *Ibid.*, p. 434. • 19, Lone Wolf: Nabokov, *op. cit.*, p. 220. • 19, White Bear: Josephy, *op. cit.*, p. 372. • 21, Frethorne: Demos, John, *Remarkable Providences* (Boston: Northeastern University Press, 1991), pp. 46-48. • 23, Bradford: Blumenthal, Shirley, and Ozer, Jerome, *Coming to America: Immigrants from the British Isles* (New York, Laurel Leaf Books, 1980), pp. 23-24. • 27, Buettner: *Narrative of Johann Carl Buettner* (New York: Fred Heartman, 1915), pp. 25-28. • 29, Equiano: Gutman, Herbert G., editor-in-chief, *"Who Built America?"* (New York: Pantheon Books, 1989), p. 67. • 31, Hamilton: Wolf, Stephanie Grauman, *As Various as Their Land* (New York: Harper Collins, 1993), p. 232. • 39, Crevecoeur: Commager, Henry Steele and Nevins, Allan, eds. *The Heritage of America* (Boston: Little, Brown, 1949), p. 354. • 41, Collin: Johnson, Amandas, ed., *The Journal and Biography of Nicholas Collin 1746-1831* (Philadelphia: The New Jersey Society of Pennsylvania, 1936), pp. 235-236. • 42, Samuel: Karp, Abraham J., *Golden Door to America: The Jewish Immigrant Experience* (New York: Penguin, 1976), p. 25. • 44, young immigrant: Allen, Leslie, *Liberty: The Statue and the American Dream* (New York: Summit Books, 1985), p. 55. • 45, De La Tour: Rae, *op. cit.*, pp. 40-41. • 47, Barlow: Gutman, *op. cit.*, p. 232. • 49, Bohning: Bohning, Ernst, "Hooray, We're Going to America," ed. by Jill Carter Knuth, reprinted with her permission, p. 2. • 51, Cummins: *The Times* (London), December 24, 1846. • 51, McNabb: Cavanah, Frances, ed., *We Came to America* (Philadelphia: Macrae Smith Company, 1954), pp. 140-141. • 52, Sweden: Veirs, Kristina, ed., *Nordic Heritage Northwest* (Seattle: The Writing Works, 1982), p.10. • 52, Norway: Cavanah, *op. cit.*, p. 195. • 52, Ireland: *Ibid.*, p. 137. • 53, "A deafening wail . . .": Schrier, Arnold, *Ireland and the American Emigration, 1850-1900* (Minneapolis: University of Minnesota Press, 1958), p. 90. • 53, Schweizer: *The Old Land and the New*, ed. and trans. by Billigmeier, Robert H. and Picard, Fred Altschuler (Minneapolis: University of Minnesota Press, 1965), p. 151. • 54, Heck: Kalergis, Mary Motley, *Home of the Brave* (New York: Dutton, 1989), p. 292. • 54, Castanis: Cavanah, *op. cit.*, p. 119. • 55, Bottomley: Taylor, Philip, *The Distant Magnet* (New York, Harper Torchbooks, 1971), p. 131. • 55, Dubach: Isely, Elise Dubach, *Sunbonnet Days* (Caldwell, ID: Caxton Printers, 1935), p. 31. • 55, Jewish girl: Sachar, Howard M., *A History of the Jews in America* (New York: Knopf, 1992), p. 41. • 57, Carnegie: Hutner, Gordon, ed., *Immigrant Voices*

(New York: Signet Books, 1999), pp. 65-68. • 57, "immortal Irish . . .": Takaki, Ronald, *A Larger Memory* (Boston: Little Brown, 1998), p. 113. • 58, Klein: Kamphoefner, Walter D. *et al.*, *News from the Land of Freedom* (Ithaca, NY: Cornell University Press, 1991), p. 389. • 59, Frank: Karp, Abraham J., *Golden Door to America: The Jewish Immigrant Experience* (New York: Penguin, 1976), pp. 50-51. • 63, Dubach: Isely, *op. cit.*, pp. 62-64. • 65, Howard: Cavanah, *op. cit.*, pp. 55-56. • 67, Ryd: Reed, Ishmael, ed., *MultiAmerica: Essays on Cultural Wars and Cultural Peace* (New York: Viking, 1997), p. 4. • 68, Schaddelee: Kalergis, *op. cit.*, p. 156. • 69, Bruemmer: Berger, Josef and Dorothy, eds., *Diary of America* (New York: Simon and Schuster, 1957), p. 222. • 69, Harkin: Hess, Jeffrey A., *Three Immigrant Stories* (Minneapolis: Minnesota Historical Society, 1977), p. 20. • 70, Kleberg: Kownslar, Allan O., *The Texans* (New York: American Heritage Publishing Co., 1972), p. 154. • 71, von Hinueber: *Ibid.*, pp. 150-151. • 71, Haidusek: Cavanah, *op. cit.*, p. 50. • 72, Evans: Edgerly, Lois Stiles, ed. & comp., *Give Us This Day: A Daybook of Women's Words* (Gardiner, ME: Tilbury House, 1990), p. 133. • 73, Holmes: *Ibid.*, p. 51. • 74, Circulars: Cavanah, *op. cit.*, p. 31. • 75, Coronel: Morefield, Richard, *The Mexican Adaptation in American California, 1846-1875* (San Francisco: R&E Research Associates, repr. 1971), p. 86-87. • 76, Norwegian miner: Adler, Mortimer J., gen. ed., *The Annals of America*, Vol. 8 (Chicago: Encyclopaedia Britannica, 1968), pp. 489-490. • 76, Schloss: Marcus, Jacob Rader, *Memoirs of American Jews, 1775-1865* Vol. 2 (Philadelphia: Jewish Publication Society, 5715/1955), pp. 264-266. • 77, Jean: Pula, James S., comp. & ed., *The French in America, 1488-1974* (Dobbs Ferry, NY: Oceana, 1975), pp. 145-146. • 79, Hunt: Hunt, Mark, *The Legacy I Leave* (Santa Ana, CA: Friis-Pioneer Press, 1984), pp. 148-149. • 81, Shaw: Cavanah, *op. cit.*, p. 63. • 82, Bloomer: Meier, Peg, ed., *Bring Warm Clothes: Letters and Photos from Minnesota's Past* (Minneapolis: Minneapolis Star and Tribune Co., 1981), pp 84, 86. • 82, Andersen: Stilling, Niels Peter and Olsen, Anne Lisbeth, eds., *A New Life: Danish Emigration to North America* (Aalborg, Denmark: Danes Worldwide Archives, 1994), pp. 64-65. • 85, Dodge: Goldstein, Richard, *Mine Eyes Have Seen* (New York, Simon and Schuster, 1997), p. 139. • 87, Bohemian girl: Berger, pp. 344-345. • 88, Senger: Sherman, William C. *et al.*, eds., *Plains Folk: North Dakota's Ethnic History* (Fargo, ND: North Dakota Institute for Regional Studies at North Dakota State University, 1988), p. 138. • 88, Raaen: Raaen, Aagot, *Grass of the Earth* (New York: Arno Press, 1979), pp. 112-113. • 89, Lindgren: Barton, H. Arnold, ed., *Letters from the Promised Land: Swedes in America, 1840-1914* (Minneapolis: University of Minnesota Press, 1975), p. 150. • 89, Czech girl: Berger, *op. cit.*, pp. 346-347. • 91, Horowitz: Banks, Ann, ed., *First-Person America* (New York: Knopf, 1980), p. 32. • 93, Harris: Rae, *op. cit.*, pp. 207-209. • 94, Pupin: Cavanah, *op. cit.*, pp. 298-300. • 95, Cristoforo: Emsden, Katharine, ed., *Coming to America: A New Life in a New Land* (Lowell, MA: Discovery Enterprises, 1993), p. 39. • 95, Kin: Kin, Huie, *Reminiscences* (Peiping,

China: San Yu Press, 1932; New York: G.L. Trigg, 1982), pp. 26-27. • 97, Lemay: Banks, *op. cit.*, p. 393. • 99, Christowe: Cavanah, *op. cit.*, pp. 21-24. • 101, Martin: Sherman, *op. cit.*, p. 133. • 102, Weichel: Coan, Peter Morton, *Ellis Island Interviews* (New York: Facts on File, 1997), p. 218. • 103, Laaksonen: Hess, *op. cit.*, p. 26. • 103, Antin: Rae, *op. cit.*, p. 49. • 103, Kyono: Ito, Kazuo, *Issei: A History of Japanese Immigrants in North America*, trans. Shinichiro Nakamura and Jean S. Gerard (Seattle: Japanese Community Service, 1973), p. 40. • 105, Adamic: Goldstein, *op. cit.*, pp. 165-166. • 109, Yokoyama: Ito, *op. cit.*, p. 192. • 109, Inouye: Luchetti, Cathy, ed., *"I Do!": Courtship, Love and Marriage on the American Frontier* (New York, Crown, 1996), p. 203. • 110, Ganz: Howe, Irving and Libo, Kenneth, eds., *How We Lived: A Documentary History of Immigrant Jews in America, 1880-1930* (New York: Richard Marek, 1979), p. 136. • 111, Corresca: Holt, Hamilton, ed., *Life Stories of Undistinguished Americans* (1906; reprint, New York: Routledge, 1990), p. 34. • 112, Dekrovich: Wright, Giles R. and Green, Howard L., eds., *Work* (Trenton, NJ: New Jersey Historical Commission, 1987), p. 37. • 112, Lithuanian: Conway, Jill Ker, *Written by Herself: Autobiographies of American Women* (New York: Vintage Books, 1992), p. 16. • 112, Frowne: Holt, *op. cit.*, p. 26. • 113, Corsi: Cavanah, *op. cit.*, p. 152. • 115, Nunes Lopes: Halter, Marilyn, *Between Race and Ethnicity: Cape Verdean American Immigrants, 1860-1965* (Urbana: University of Illinois Press, 1993), pp. 114-115. • 117, Gollup: Cohen, Rose, *Out of the Shadow: A Russian Jewish Girlhood on the Lower East Side* (Ithaca, NY: Cornell University Press, 1995), p. 154. • 118, Beame: Coan, *op. cit.*, p. 76. • 119, Karavolas: *Ibid.*, p. 279. • 120, Chinese immigrant: Daniels, Roger, *Asian America* (Seattle: University of Washington Press, 1988), p. 70. • 121, Kojimo: Namias, June, *First Generation* (Boston: Beacon Press, 1978), p. 130. • 121, Orite: Sarasohn, Eileen Sunada, ed., *The Issei: Portrait of a Pioneer* (Palo Alto, CA: Pacific Books, 1983), p. 123. • 122, Tovas: Coan, *op. cit.*, p. 287. • 123, Colbert: Benjamin, Robert Spiers, ed., *I Am an American* (Freeport, NY: Books for Libraries Press, 1941, repr. 1970), p. 122. • 124, Hungarian girl: Kalergis, *op. cit.*, p. 332. • 125, social worker: Balch, Emily Greene, *Our Slavic Fellow Citizens* (New York: Arno Press, 1969), p. 359. • 128, Jastrow: Macleod, David I., *The Age of the Child: Children in America, 1890-1920* (New York: Twayne Publishers, 1998), p. 88. • 129, Chicago boy: *Ibid.*, p. 91. • 129, Polish immigrant: Takaki, *op. cit.*, pp. 225-227. • 130, Walinsky: Morrison, Joan, and Zabusky, Charlotte Fox, *American Mosaic: the Immigrant Experience in the Words of Those Who Lived It* (Pittsburgh: University of Pittsburgh Press, 1980), p. 1. • 131, Yolles: Spiers, *op. cit.*, p. 49. • 131, Mardikian: Kulhanjian, Gary A., *An Abstract of the Historical and Sociological Aspects of Armenian Immigration to the United States, 1890-1930* (San Francisco: R & E Research Associates, 1975), p. 59. • 133, Dache: Cavanah, *op. cit.*, pp. 89-91. • 135, Assibian: Coan, *op. cit.*, p. 403. • 137, Lugosi: *Ibid.*, p. 369. • 137, Cassidy: Wright, Giles R., ed., *The Journey from Home* (Trenton, NJ: New Jersey Historical Commission, 1986), p. 21.

• 139, Arnold: Wright, *Journey, op. cit.*, pp. 119-120. • 141, Nickerson: *From Flappers to Flivvers . . . We Helped Make the 20s Roar* (Greendale, WI: Reminisce Books, n.d.), p. 153. • 143, Vallangca: Vallangca, Robert V., comp., *Pinoy: The First Wave* (San Francisco: Strawberry Hill Press, 1977), pp. 169-170. • 145, Spanos: Coan, *op. cit.*, p. 290. • 149, Akimoto: Goldstein, *op. cit.*, p. 283. • 151, Stimler: Wright, Giles R., ed., *Looking Back* (Trenton, NJ: New Jersey Historical Commission, 1986), pp. 50-53. • 152, Simic: Aciman, Andre, ed., *Letters of Transit: Reflections on Exile, Identity, Language, and Loss* (New York: W.W. Norton, 1999), p. 119. • 153, Lapsins: Wright, Giles R., ed., *Arrival and Settlement in a New Place*, Trenton, NJ: New Jersey Historical Commission, 1986), p. 19. • 153, Torini: Coan, *op. cit.*, pp. 59-60. • 155, Rosario: Wright, Giles R. ed., *Schooling and Education* (Trenton, NJ: New Jersey Historical Commission, 1987), p. 24. • 156, Graff: Wright, *Arrival and Settlement, op. cit.*, p. 32. • 157, Mishan: Wright, *The Journey from Home, op. cit.*, pp. 14-15, 17. • 159, Pacheco: personal communication. • 160, Kennedy: "Three Decades of Mass Immigration: The Legacy of the 1965 Immigration Act" from *Bulletin of the Center for Immigration Studies*, September 1995. • 160, Johnson: *Ibid.*, p. 2. • 161, Shanti: Takaki, *op. cit.*, p. 283. • 162, Yang: Editors of Time-Life Books, *Immigrants: the New Americans* (Alexandria, VA: Time-Life Books, 1999), p. 166. • 163, Lev: Wright, *The Journey from Home, op. cit.*, pp. 17-18. • 164, Arias: personal interview. • 167, Golden Venture Woman: Chin, Ko-Lin, *Smuggled Chinese: Clandestine Immigration to the United States* (Philadelphia: Temple University Press, 1999), p. 10. • 168, Illegal from North Africa: personal interview. • 170, Carrera: personal interview. • 171, Liberman: personal interview. • 172, Tabotabo: Wright, *Looking Back, op. cit.*, pp. 55-56. • 173, Jorge: Gonzalez-Pando, Miguel, *The Cuban Americans* (Westport, CT: Greenwood Press, 1998), p. 129. • 175, Mar: *Paper Daughter: A Memoir* (New York: HarperCollins, 1999), pp. 57-58. • 176, Romero: Reed, *op. cit.*, pp. 90-91. • 177, Korean immigrant: Moon, H. Jo, *Korean Immigrants and the Challenge of Adjustment* (Westport, CT: Greenwood Press, 1999) • 179, Dominican woman: Foner, Nancy, ed., *New Immigrants in New York* (New York: Columbia University Press, 1987), p. 20. • 180, Inugu: Kalergis, *op. cit.*, p. 240. • 180, Phon: Steltzer, Ulli, *The New Americans: Immigrant Life in Southern California* (Pasadena: New Sage Press, 1988), p. 18. • 181, Rosario: personal interview. • 182, Saleh: Steltzer, *op. cit.*, p. 71. • 183, Singh: *Ibid.*, p. 72. • 184, Aronov: personal interview. • 185, del Rosario: personal interview. • 185, Soviet Jewish immigrant: Ashabranner, Brent, *The New Americans: Changing Patterns in U.S. Immigration* (New York: Dodd, Mead, 1983), p. 139. • 186, Pereira: Takaki, Ronald, *Strangers from a Different Shore: A History of Asian Americans* (Boston: Little Brown, 1998), pp. 85-86. • 186, Chou: Steltzer, *op. cit.*, p. 132. • 186, Mohanty: Editors of Time-Life Books, *op. cit.*, p. 158. • 187, Sidi: Kalergis, *op. cit.*, p. 115. • 187, Arias: Editors of Time-Life Books, *op. cit.*, p. 156. • 187, Nguyen: *Ibid.*, p. 160. • 187, Mehari: Kalergis, *op. cit.*, p. 81.